SCHOLASTIC Pocket
World Atlas

SCHOLASTIC REFERENCE

An imprint of

SCHOLASTIC

Library of Congress Cataloging-in-Publication Data
Steele, Philip, 1948–
Scholastic atlas of the world/by Philip Steele
p.cm.
Includes index.
1. Atlases [1. Atlases. 2. Geography.] I. Title.
G1021.S687 2001
912—dc21   00-030064

ISBN 0-439-68193-6

Produced by Miles Kelly Publishing Ltd
Bardfield Centre, Great Bardfield,
Essex, CM7 4SL, UK

Publishing Director: Anne Marshall
Art Director: Jo Brewer
Senior Editor: Jenni Rainford
Cartography: Digital Wisdom (Nicholas Rowland)
Consultant: Clive Carpenter

Additional Text: Philip Steele
Statistics: Clive Carpenter
Index: Hannah Todd
Picture Research: Hannah Todd, Liberty Newton

Color Reproduction: DPI Colour Digital,
Saffron Walden, Essex, UK

10 9 8 7 6 5 4 3 2 1
05 06 07 08 09
First printing, July 2005
Printed in the U.S.A.   23

Scholastic Reference Staff

Editorial Director: Kenneth R. Wright
Editor: Mary Varilla Jones
Assistant Editors: Elysa Jacobs, Brenda Murray
Curriculum Consultant: Bob Stremme
Flag Consultant: Dr. Whitney Smith, Flag
Research Center

Creative Director: David Saylor
Art Director: Nancy Sabato

Managing Editor: Karyn Browne
Production Editor: Melinda Weigel

Manufacturing Vice President: Angela Biola
Manufacturing Managers: Kirk Howle,
                    Heidi Robinson

The population statistics used in this book are
based on figures from census departments or
UN estimates.

Credits
The publishers would like to thank the following sources for the use of their photographs:
Page 12 (TR) Galen Rowell/CORBIS; 13 (TL) Hanan Isachar/CORBIS; 13 (C) James L. Amos/CORBIS;
34 Kevin Fleming/CORBIS; 36 Larry Minden/FLPA; 68 Peter M. Wilson/CORBIS;
92 Derek Croucher/CORBIS; 102 Macduff Everton/CORBIS; 104 SETBOUN/CORBIS;
108 Tibor Bognár/CORBIS; 110 Raymond Gehman/CORBIS; 118 Caroline Penn/CORBIS;
130 Chris Hellier/CORBIS; 132 K.M. Westermann/CORBIS; 134 Brian A. Vikander/CORBIS;
146 Rob Howard/CORBIS; 170 Caroline Penn/CORBIS; 172 Jim Zuckerman/CORBIS;
176 Ron Watts/CORBIS; 186 New Line Productions/Pictorial Press

All other photographs from MKP Archives (Corbis, Corel, digitalSTOCK, digitalvision, PhotoDisc,
PhotoEssentials) and NASA. In addition, the publisher would like to thank Rob Jakeway and Martin Saunders
for their illustrations. Cover photo credit: RubberBall Productions/PictureQuest

The publisher has made every effort to contact all copyright holders but apologizes if any source remains unacknowledged.

A tour of the world

skyscraper cities

bustling harbors

towering mountains

Contents

How to Use This Atlas

Inside this pocket atlas you can explore the countries of the world—and learn about the people who live there.

Understanding the maps
This simple key shows you the different features, labels, and symbols that have been included in the maps. These will help you to understand them.

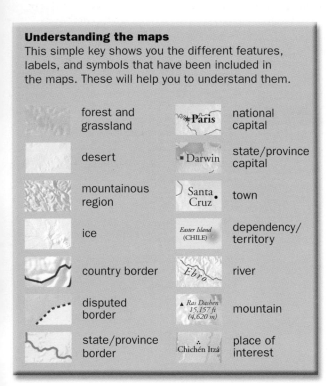

	forest and grassland	*Paris	national capital	
	desert	Darwin	state/province capital	
	mountainous region	Santa Cruz	town	
	ice	Easter Island (CHILE)	dependency/ territory	
	country border	Ebro	river	
	disputed border	Ras Dashen 15,157 ft (4,620 m)	mountain	
	state/province border	Chichén Itzá	place of interest	

Important words
Some difficult words are explained in detail in the glossary.

Photos and captions
On most spreads you will find a photo of one of the countries. The caption beneath each photo will explain where it is.

Discover more
Some amazing things you never knew about a country or state are contained in these fact boxes.

Search and find
If you want to find a city or area on the map, use the grid references to locate its exact position on the map.

Abbreviations

B.C.E.	Before Common Era	in	inch
C.E.	Common Era	l	liter
FED.	Federation	lb	pound
MTS	mountains	kg	kilogram
St.	Saint	km	kilometer
cm	centimeter	m	meter
cu	cubic	mi	mile
ft	feet	mm	millimeter
		sq	square

Political map

This identification map shows the countries and how they relate to the surrounding land area.

Geographical features box

Easy-to-recognize colored icons show you where some of the world's highest mountains and longest rivers are—as well as where the world's largest desert is. The box gives some essential information.

Country listing

Every country featured on the page is listed in order of its physical size.

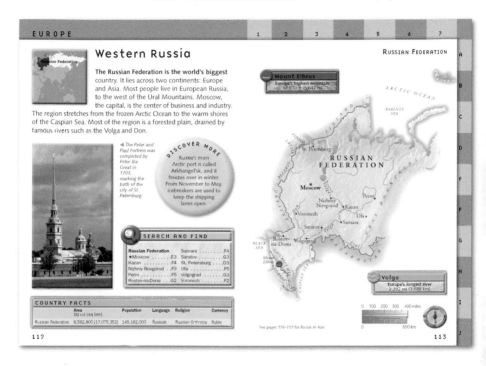

Western Russia

RUSSIAN FEDERATION

The Russian Federation is the world's biggest country. It lies across two continents: Europe and Asia. Most people live in European Russia, to the west of the Ural Mountains. Moscow, the capital, is the center of business and industry. The region stretches from the frozen Arctic Ocean to the warm shores of the Caspian Sea. Most of the region is a forested plain, drained by famous rivers such as the Volga and Don.

Mount Elbrus
Europe's highest mountain
18,510 ft (5,642 m)

◄ The Peter and Paul Fortress was completed by Peter the Great in 1703, marking the birth of the city of St. Petersburg.

DISCOVER MORE
Russia's main Arctic port is called Arkhangel'sk, and it freezes over in winter. From November to May, icebreakers are used to keep the shipping lanes open.

SEARCH AND FIND

Russian Federation		Samara F4
★Moscow E3	Saratov G3
Kazan F4	St. Petersburg D3
Nizhniy Novgorod . .F3	Ufa F5
Perm F5	Volgograd G3
Rostov-na-Donu . . .G2	Voronezh F2

Volga
Europe's longest river
2,292 mi (3,688 km)

COUNTRY FACTS

	Area sq mi (sq km)	Population	Language	Religion	Currency
Russian Federation	6,592,800 (17,075,352)	145,182,000	Russian	Russian Orthodox	Ruble

See pages 116–117 for Russia in Asia.

0 100 200 300 400 miles
0 650 km

112   113

Fact boxes

You can use these statistics to discover a country's area, population, language, religion, and currency. On the continent spreads you will find the largest country by area and population within that continent. For the United States and Canada, you can find out state, province, and territory information.

Physical maps

On these maps you can find the towns where most people live as well as some areas that are important for other reasons, such as trade and tourism. The longest rivers, the highest mountains, and the most notable physical features are also shown.

Scale and compass rose

The scale allows you to find out how large an area on a map is. The compass rose shows you the direction of north.

5

Making Maps

About 4,500 years ago a skilled worker in Babylon was making detailed markings on a clay tablet. The markings he made probably showed some buildings in a nearby river valley. The worker was making one of the very first maps. Today, most of our maps are produced by computers. Material is collected from surveys of Earth, aerial photos, and satellite images. Computers arrange this material to draw the highly accurate maps you use today.

▲ This is what Venice, Italy, looks like when it is photographed from space.

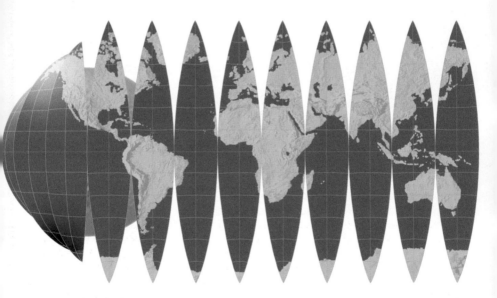

Peeling the orange

If you could peel off Earth's surface just like the skin of an orange, you would be left with segments similar to those shown here. Mapmakers who use this process, fill the gaps between the segments by digitally stretching them so that they form a flat surface.

6

What is a projection?

Because Earth is round, mapmakers have a very difficult job representing it on a flat map. They have to stretch and distort Earth to make it appear flat on a page. The way in which Earth is stretched so it can appear on one page is called a map projection, and each projection stretches the image of Earth in a different way. There are many types of map projection, and the ones shown below are most commonly used. Some map projections show the shape of the land accurately but distort the size. With others, the opposite is true. However, no map projection is completely accurate, and all of them distort to some extent.

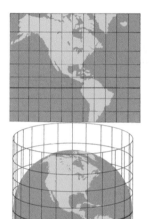

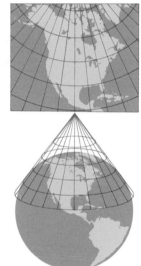

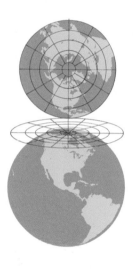

Cylinder shaped

Imagine wrapping a sheet of paper around a lit-up globe of the world and projecting the lines of latitude and longitude (see page 9) onto the paper. Unwrap the paper and spread it flat out to produce the kind of flat map often used by sailors.

Cone shaped

Imagine placing a paper cone over a lit-up globe, and projecting the lines of latitude and longitude onto the cone. Unwrap and flatten it to produce the kind of map that shows wide areas of land, such as the United States or Russia.

Plane shaped

Imagine holding a sheet of paper so that it touches one place on a lit-up globe. Project the lines of latitude and longitude onto the paper and then lay it on a flat surface. This kind of map is often used to show the world's polar regions.

Using Maps

A map is a picture of an area on Earth's surface. It uses lines, colors, and symbols to give you information about that area. It may be a picture of the whole world or of a small area in a city or town. Maps tell you many different things—the location of countries, cities, and towns, the features of the landscape, the distribution of the population, or the climate of a particular region.

All about scale

The area shown on a map is, of course, much bigger than it appears on the printed page—this is because the map is drawn to scale. A map of the world shows us only a small amount of detail—we call it a small-scale map. A street map may show details of every building—it is called a large-scale map.

How to use a map scale

1 To measure the distance between two cities, first mark the positions of the city dots onto the edge of a small piece of paper.

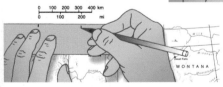

2 Place the paper along the map's scale, with the left-hand mark against the 0. If the scale is shorter than the distance you want to measure, mark where the scale ends, say 200 mi (320 km). Take a note of the distance you have already measured. Place this new mark against the 0.

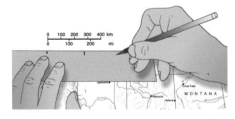

3 Repeat this last step until you have reached the mark for the second city. Then add up each of the distances. This will give you the correct total distance between the two cities.

Finding the location of a place

Maps are marked with a system of lines to help you describe and find the location of a certain place. The horizontal lines are called lines of latitude, and the vertical ones are lines of longitude. Latitude and longitude are measured in degrees (°).

Lines of latitude

These are imaginary lines that circle the world in an east–west direction. They tell you how far north or south a place is from the Equator (a line drawn at 0° latitude). They are drawn parallel to the Equator. Two special lines of latitude are the Tropic of Cancer and the Tropic of Capricorn. The Tropic of Cancer marks the northern boundary of the tropics. The Tropic of Capricorn marks the southern boundary. Because these regions lie close to the Equator, it is very hot, as the Sun shines directly overhead.

line of latitude

Tropic of Cancer
Equator
Tropic of Capricorn

Lines of longitude

These are imaginary lines that run across Earth's surface in a north–south direction, from the North Pole to the South Pole. We start counting lines of longitude to the east and the west of the Greenwich Meridian, the 0° line of longitude that passes through the borough of Greenwich in London, England.

line of longitude

Hemispheres

The Greenwich Meridian and the 180° Meridian divide the world into two halves called the Eastern Hemisphere and the Western Hemisphere— each hemisphere has 180 degrees of longitude.

Western Hemisphere

180° Meridian

Eastern Hemisphere

The Equator divides the world into two halves called the Northern Hemisphere and the Southern Hemisphere—each hemisphere has 90 degrees of latitude.

Northern Hemisphere

Equator

Southern Hemisphere

On a map you can find any place on Earth's surface if you know its latitude and its longitude. For example, the exact location of the city of Philadelphia, Pennsylvania, U.S.A., is as follows: 40°N, 75°W. In other words, Philadelphia lies on the line of latitude which is 40 degrees north of the Equator, and on the line of longitude 75 degrees west of the Greenwich Meridian.

Earth in Space

Earth is part of a family of planets, moons, comets, asteroids,
and other space material traveling around the Sun. We call this family
the solar system (after the Latin word *sol*, which means "the Sun").
The Sun is a small star, one of millions in an enormous star group
called the Milky Way. We belong to this galaxy, which is just one of
millions of others in the vast universe.

The planets

Some of the planets, such as Earth and Mars, are
made mainly of rock. Others are made of gas and are
much bigger than our planet Earth. We sometimes call
them the gas giants. Pluto, the smallest planet, is a
mixture of ice and rock. Earth is the only one of the
nine planets on which we know for sure that life exists.

Saturn

Sun

Mars

Venus

Jupiter

Earth

Mercury

The spinning Earth

Earth turns around on its axis like a spinning top. This axis is an imaginary line between the North and South poles. It takes 24 hours for Earth to spin all the way around, giving us day and night. As Earth spins, it is daytime in places facing the Sun, and nighttime in places facing away from the Sun. At the same time, Earth is also moving around the Sun.

Neptune

Pluto

Uranus

Earth's orbit

The tilted angle of Earth's axis and Earth's orbit around the Sun give us our seasons. From March to September, Earth's Northern Hemisphere is tilted toward the Sun. Places in the Northern Hemisphere have spring, followed by summer. At the same time, places in the Southern Hemisphere have fall, followed by winter. From September to March the Southern Hemisphere is tilted toward the Sun. Places in the Southern Hemisphere have spring and summer, while those in the Northern Hemisphere have fall and winter.

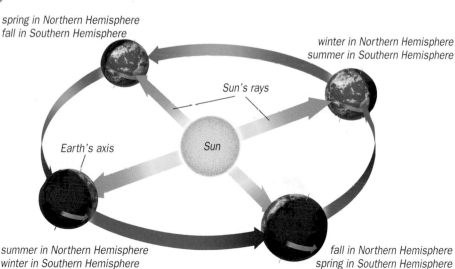

spring in Northern Hemisphere
fall in Southern Hemisphere

winter in Northern Hemisphere
summer in Southern Hemisphere

Sun's rays

Earth's axis

Sun

summer in Northern Hemisphere
winter in Southern Hemisphere

fall in Northern Hemisphere
spring in Southern Hemisphere

Our Planet Earth

About 73 per cent of our planet is covered with water. The Pacific Ocean, the largest body of water, covers almost one-third of Earth's surface. The remaining land is divided up into today's seven great continents—from largest to smallest: Asia, Africa, North America, South America, Antarctica, Europe, and Oceania. The landscape is dotted with a huge variety of wonderful natural features: towering mountains and hot, dry deserts, fast-flowing rivers and large lakes, majestic volcanoes and steep-sided valleys, caves and caverns many miles underground, huge rivers of ice called glaciers, and vast ice sheets.

▲ **Highest mountain**
Mount Everest is on the border of Nepal and China. Scientists have recently discovered that it's even bigger than they previously thought! In November 1999 the mountain's official height was changed to 29,028 ft (8,848 m) —that's 7 ft (2 m) more than its previous official height.

▲ **Largest ocean**
The Pacific Ocean is almost double the size of the Atlantic, covering 64,186,300 sq mi (1,662,425,000 sq km).

▶ **Largest lake**
Asia's Caspian Sea covers an area of 152,239 sq mi (394,299 sq km). Although it is landlocked, which means it is surrounded by land on all sides, the Romans called it a "sea" because its waters are salty. The world's largest freshwater lake is Lake Superior, one of North America's five Great Lakes.

▲ **Largest desert**
The Sahara Desert covers almost one-third of the huge continent of Africa. Its surface measures a total of 1.35 million sq mi (3.5 million sq km). Only 30 per cent is sand and sand dunes; the rest of the desert consists of broad flat areas of small rocks and gravel.

▲ **Lowest place**
The Dead Sea makes up part of the border between Israel and Jordan. It lies at 1,312 ft (400 m) below sea level. It is called the Dead Sea because no fish and only a few kinds of plants can survive in its very salty waters.

▲ **Longest river**
Africa's mighty Nile River flows for 4,145 mi (6,670 km) from its source near Lake Victoria northward to the Mediterranean Sea. By contrast, the world's shortest recorded river is the Roe in the state of Montana—it's just 201 ft (64 m) long!

▲ **Largest island**
Greenland is more than four times the size of the second-largest island, Papua New Guinea. The ice-cold land of Greenland covers an area of 840,000 sq mi (2,175,600 sq km). It is a dependency of Denmark and is about 50 times bigger than Denmark itself.

Population explosion

There are now more than six billion people living on Earth. However, the population is not evenly distributed, as some larger countries have small populations.

Area and population

Australia covers almost 3 million sq mi (7.8 million sq km), yet it has a population of just 18.8 million. The Netherlands is just 16,033 sq mi (41,525 sq km), yet its population is almost as big as that of Australia—15.8 million.

Netherlands   **Australia**

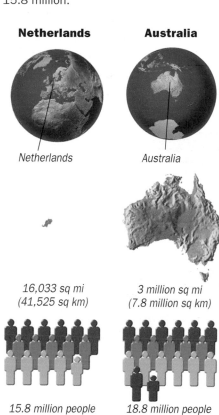

Netherlands   *Australia*

16,033 sq mi   *3 million sq mi*
(41,525 sq km)   *(7.8 million sq km)*

15.8 million people   *18.8 million people*

The Moving Earth

Earth is a huge rocky ball. Large chunks of land called continents and vast expanses of ocean cover its surface. They are part of the hard "skin," or crust, that surrounds the whole Earth. Beneath this crust are layers of hot rocks and metals, some of them solid and some liquid. Immediately below the crust is a layer of hard rock called the mantle. Below the mantle is the next layer, called the outer core. Here it is so hot that the rocks have melted and become liquid. Farther down still, at the very center of Earth, lies a solid ball— the inner core.

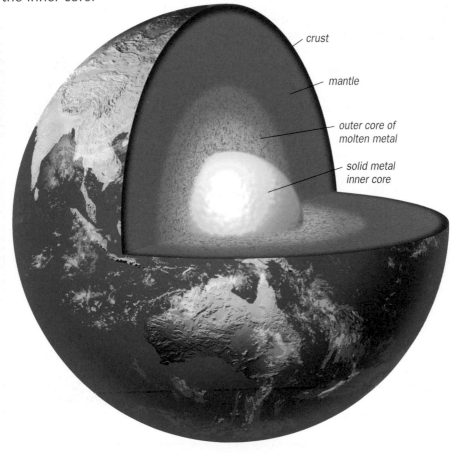

crust

mantle

outer core of molten metal

solid metal inner core

Plate movement

Earth's crust is made up of plates. These sometimes move away from each other, and even toward each other. They also slide past each other. When two plates collide, one plate may pile up against the other to form a great mountain range, such as the Andes in South America. This mountain building does not happen quickly, though—it takes millions of years. After a collision, one plate might be forced down below the other to form a deep trench on the ocean floor.

crack in Earth's crust (fault line)

sliding motion causes rocks to strain

The changing Earth

Over hundreds of millions of years, planet Earth has changed shape and structure, from one giant land mass to the individual continents we know today.

200 million years ago

The world consisted of a huge single landmass, Pangaea, which began to break apart slowly. The very biggest dinosaurs roamed the land, and the first birds appeared. Shelled squid, snails, and many kinds of fish lived in the warm seas.

120 million years ago

The breakup of the supercontinent Pangaea produced two smaller landmasses—Laurasia to the north and Gondwana to the south. The first flowering plants appeared on the land, and dinosaurs developed spiky horns and body armor.

60 million years ago

Laurasia and Gondwana eventually broke up to form the seven continents we know today. By this time the last dinosaurs had died out, and warm-blooded mammals were becoming common.

Where in the World

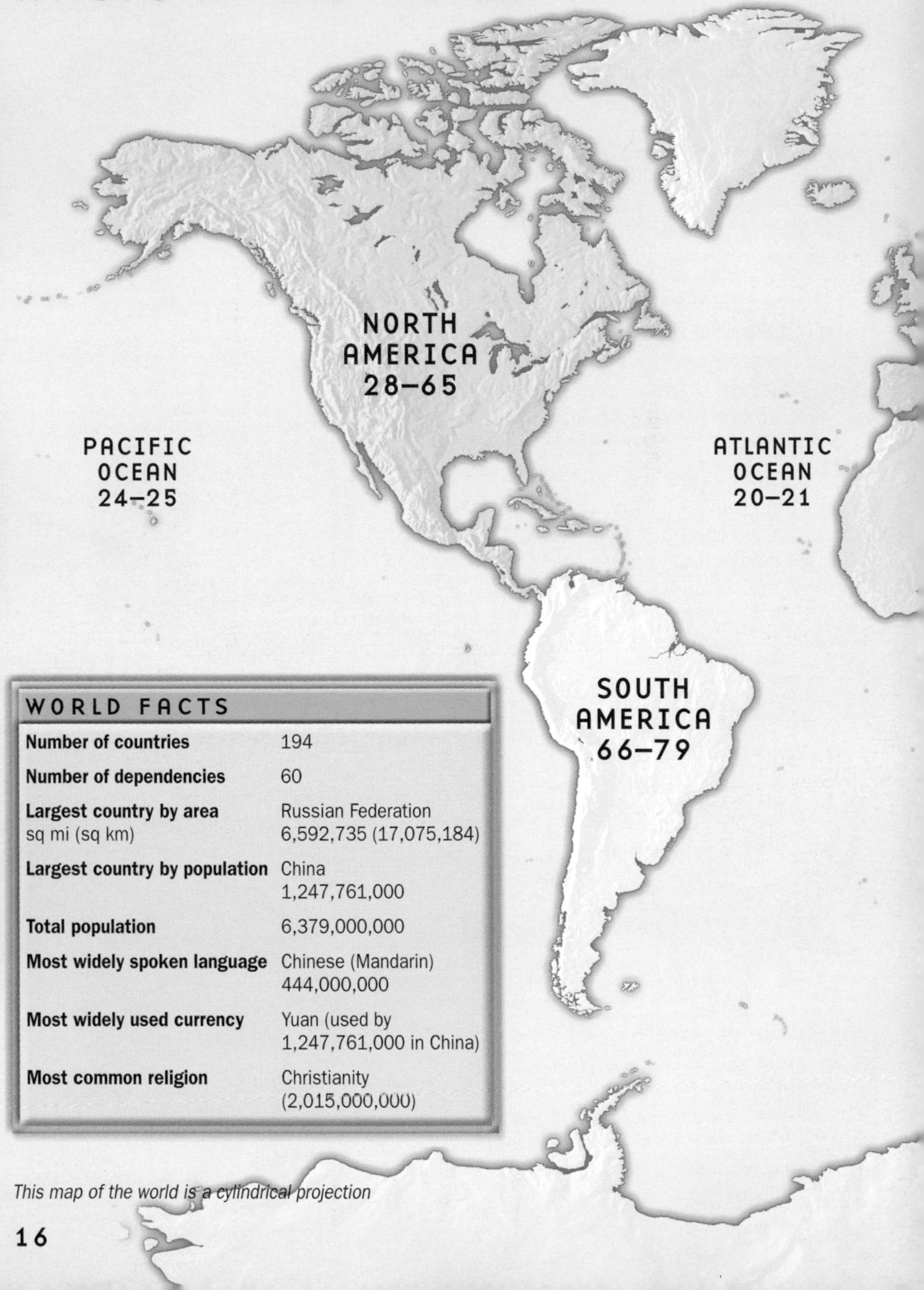

NORTH AMERICA
28–65

PACIFIC OCEAN
24–25

ATLANTIC OCEAN
20–21

SOUTH AMERICA
66–79

WORLD FACTS

Number of countries	194
Number of dependencies	60
Largest country by area sq mi (sq km)	Russian Federation 6,592,735 (17,075,184)
Largest country by population	China 1,247,761,000
Total population	6,379,000,000
Most widely spoken language	Chinese (Mandarin) 444,000,000
Most widely used currency	Yuan (used by 1,247,761,000 in China)
Most common religion	Christianity (2,015,000,000)

This map of the world is a cylindrical projection

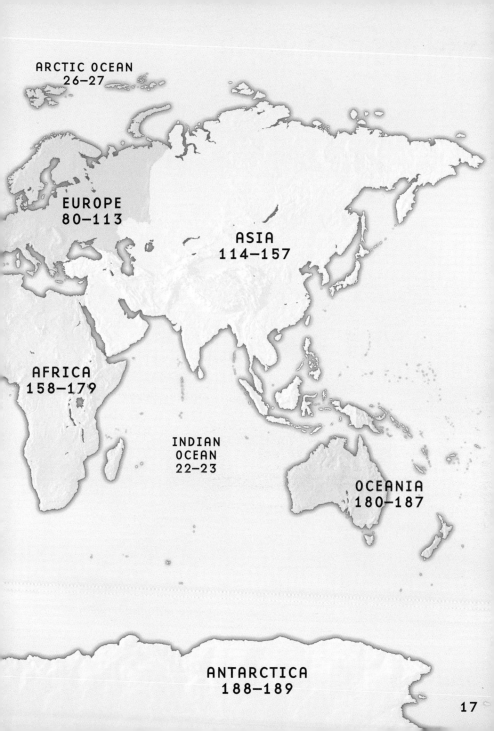

ARCTIC OCEAN
26–27

EUROPE
80–113

ASIA
114–157

AFRICA
158–179

INDIAN
OCEAN
22–23

OCEANIA
180–187

ANTARCTICA
188–189

The Physical World

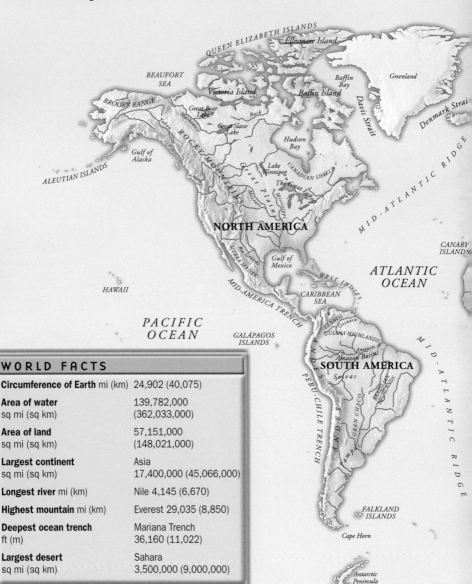

QUEEN ELIZABETH ISLANDS

Ellesmere Island

BEAUFORT
SEA

BROOKS RANGE

Victoria Island

*Baffin
Bay*

Baffin Island

Greenland

*Great Bear
Lake*

Back

Mackenzie

*Great Slave
Lake*

Yukon

R O C K Y   M O U N T A I N S

Davis Strait

Denmark Strait

*Hudson
Bay*

Gulf of
Alaska

CANADIAN SHIELD

*Lake
Winnipeg*

Great Plains

MID-ATLANTIC RIDGE

ALEUTIAN ISLANDS

The Great Lakes

Missouri

Mississippi

NORTH AMERICA

CANARY
ISLANDS

SIERRA MADRE

Rio Grande

Gulf of
Mexico

WEST INDIES

**ATLANTIC
OCEAN**

HAWAII

MID-AMERICA TRENCH

CARIBBEAN
SEA

*PACIFIC
OCEAN*

GALÁPAGOS
ISLANDS

LLANOS

Orinoco

GUIANA HIGHLANDS

A N D E S

Amazon

Amazon Basin

SOUTH AMERICA

Selvas

M I D - A T L A N T I C   R I D G E

PERU-CHILE TRENCH

GRAN CHACO

*BRAZILIAN
HIGHLANDS*

Pampas

FALKLAND
ISLANDS

Cape Horn

*Antarctic
Peninsula*

WORLD FACTS

Circumference of Earth mi (km)	24,902 (40,075)
Area of water sq mi (sq km)	139,782,000 (362,033,000)
Area of land sq mi (sq km)	57,151,000 (148,021,000)
Largest continent sq mi (sq km)	Asia 17,400,000 (45,066,000)
Longest river mi (km)	Nile 4,145 (6,670)
Highest mountain mi (km)	Everest 29,035 (8,850)
Deepest ocean trench ft (m)	Mariana Trench 36,160 (11,022)
Largest desert sq mi (sq km)	Sahara 3,500,000 (9,000,000)

This map of the world is a cylindrical projection

ARCTIC OCEAN

SEVERNAYA ZEMLYA

NOVAYA ZEMLYA

NEW SIBERIAN
ISLANDS

LAPTEV SEA

EAST
SIBERIAN
SEA

KARA
SEA

BARENTS
SEA

Lapland

NORWEGIAN
SEA

Central
Siberian
Plateau

BERING
SEA

Siberian
Lowland

Yenisey

Nizhnyaya Tunguska

Lena

Aldan

URAL MOUNTAINS

Dvina

Ob

NORTH
SEA

BALTIC SEA

Valga

EUROPEAN PLAIN

EUROPE

ASIA

Yenisey

Ob

Angara

Lena

Amur

SEA OF
OKHOTSK

Dnieper

Ural

Lake
Baykal

Volga

CASPIAN SEA

SAYAN MTS.

KURIL TRENCH

CARPATHIAN
MTS

ALPS

Danube

BLACK SEA

ARAL
SEA

Lake Balkhash

Gobi
Desert

SEA OF
JAPAN

Turanian
Plateau

TIEN MTS

Huang He

MEDITERRANEAN SEA

Tigris

ZAGROS MTS

HINDU KUSH

KUNLAN MTS

Tibetan
Plateau

Chang Jiang

EAST CHINA
SEA

PACIFIC
OCEAN

ATLAS MTS

Euphrates

Indus

HIMALAYA

Huang He

MICRONESIA

Sahara

Niger

Nile

RED SEA

Nubian
Desert

Arabian
Peninsula

ARABIAN
SEA

DECCAN

Ganges

Bay of
Bengal

Irrawaddy

SOUTH
CHINA
SEA

PHILIPPINE
SEA

AFRICA

Gulf of Aden

Mekong

Gulf of
Guinea

Ethiopian
Highlands

Urle

E A S T

CELEBES
SEA

MELANESIA

OCEANIA

Congo

GREAT RIFT VALLEY

Lake
Victoria

I N D I E S

CONGO
BASIN

Kasai

MID-INDIAN RIDGE

JAVA TRENCH

CORAL
SEA

WALVIS RIDGE

Kalahari
Desert

INDIAN
OCEAN

Great Sandy
Desert

Orange

Great Victorian
Desert

Murray

Darling

GREAT DIVIDING RANGE

Cape of
Good Hope

Great Australian
Bight

TASMAN
SEA

SOUTHWEST INDIAN RIDGE

SOUTHEAST INDIAN RIDGE

ANTARCTICA

19

Atlantic Ocean
and Islands

The Atlantic is the second-largest ocean in the world, covering an area of about 31,744,015 sq mi (82,217,000 sq km). Around its coasts are large inlets such as the Gulf of Mexico, and seas such as the Caribbean, North, Baltic, and Mediterranean. The Mid-Atlantic Ridge is an underwater mountain range. It is formed around a great crack in the ocean floor, which runs from north to south. Its route is marked by a chain of volcanic islands between Iceland and Tristan da Cunha.

▲ *The Atlantic Ocean has few islands; the majority are found in the Caribbean region.*

DISCOVER MORE

The islanders of Tristan da Cunha live in one of the world's most remote places. Their home is 1,513 mi (2,435 km) from St. Helena and 1,702 mi (2,740 km) from Africa.

SEARCH AND FIND

Ascension Island . . .F5	Iceland C5
Azores D4	Madeira E5
Bermuda E3	Newfoundland D3
Bioko F6	St. Helena G5
Bouvet Island H6	São Tomé &
British Isles D5	Príncipe F5
Canary Islands E5	South Georgia H4
Cape Verde E4	South Sandwich
Faeroe Islands C5	Islands I5
Falkland Islands . .H3	Tristan da Cunha . .G5
Greenland C4	

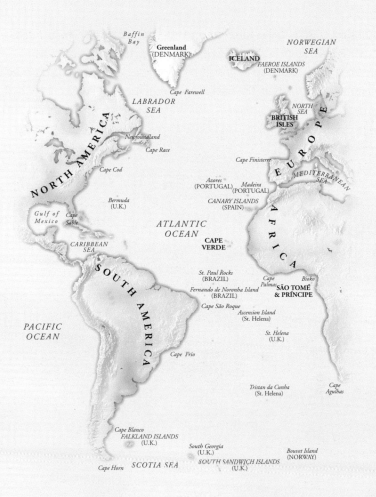

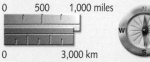

Indian Ocean
and Islands

The Indian Ocean is the third largest in the world, covering an area of about 28,350,500 sq mi (73,427,000 sq km). Its biggest islands are Madagascar, Sri Lanka, Sumatra, Java, and Borneo, beyond which lies the Pacific Ocean. The Indian Ocean meets with the Atlantic off the coast of South Africa. Corals grow in its warm waters. Coral remains have created reefs and small islands. Ocean winds called monsoons cause heavy seasonal rains in India and Southeast Asia.

DISCOVER MORE

Monsoon rains that come from the Indian Ocean are the heaviest on Earth. The island of Réunion received the rainfall record for one day—74 inches (1,870 mm).

SEARCH AND FIND

Amsterdam Island .G5
Andaman Islands . .D5
Chagos Archipelago.E4
Christmas Island . .E6
Cocos (Keeling)
  Islands F6
Comoros E2
Crozet Islands H3
Kerguelen Islands .H4
Laccadive Islands .D4
Madagascar F3

Maldives D5
Mauritius F3
Nicobar Islands . . .D5
Prince Edward
  Islands H2
Réunion F3
St. Paul Island H5
Seychelles E3
Socotra D3
Sri Lanka D5

COUNTRY FACTS

	Area sq mi (sq km)	Population	Language	Religion	Currency
Madagascar	226,656 (587,039)	15,692,000	Malagasy	Indigenous beliefs	Franc
Sri Lanka	25,332 (65,610)	19,410,000	Sinhali	Buddhist	Rupee
Mauritius	788 (2,041)	1,210,000	English	Hindu	Rupee
Comoros	719 (1,862)	509,000	Arabic	Sunni Muslim	Franc
Seychelles	176 (456)	77,000	English	Catholic	Rupee
Maldives	116 (300)	270,000	Divehi	Sunni Muslim	Rufiyaa

INDIAN OCEAN

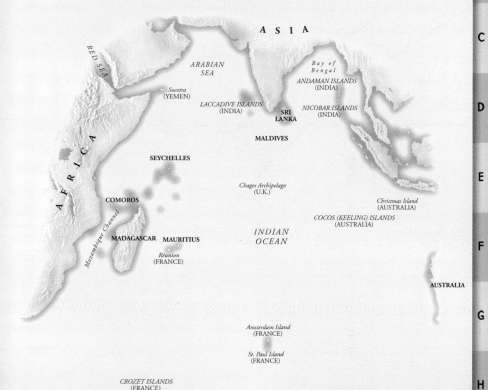

Pacific Ocean
and Islands

The **Pacific Ocean is Earth's** largest ocean. It lies between Asia and Australia in the west and the Americas in the east. It covers an area of about 64,186,300 sq mi (1,662,425,000 sq km). "Pacific" means "peaceful," but the Pacific Ocean is circled by the Ring of Fire, which is a zone of volcanoes and earthquakes.

COUNTRY FACTS

	Area sq mi (sq km)	Population	Language	Religion	Currency
Papua New Guinea	178,703 (462,841)	5,191,000	PE*/English	Catholic/Lutheran	Kina
Solomon Islands	10,985 (28,451)	409,000	English/PE*	Anglican	Dollar
Fiji	7,054 (18,270)	856,000	Fijian/English/Hindi	Hindu/Methodist	Dollar
Vanuatu	4,707 (12,191)	187,000	Bislama	Presbyterian	Vatu
Samoa	1,104 (2,859)	172,000	Samoan	Mormon/Cong**	Tala
Kiribati	313 (811)	84,500	English/Kiribati	Catholic	A Dollar††
Tonga	289 (749)	99,000	Tongan	Free Wesleyan	Pa'anga
Micronesia	271 (702)	107,000	English/Chuukese	Catholic/Cong**	US Dollar
Palau	188 (487)	19,000	Palauan/English	Catholic/Trad***	US Dollar
Marshall Islands	70 (181)	51,000	Marshallese/English	Cong*/NR†/Catholic	US Dollar
Nauru	21 (54)	12,000	Nauruan	Cong**	A Dollar††
Tuvalu	10 (26)	9,600	Tuvaluan	Church of Tuvalu	A Dollar††

*Pidgin English   **Congregational   ***Traditional beliefs   †Non-religious   ††Australian Dollar

PACIFIC OCEAN

BERING SEA

*ALEUTIAN ISLANDS
(U.S.A.)*

ASIA

NORTH AMERICA

*MIDWAY ISLANDS
(U.S.A.)*

*Wake Island
(U.S.A.)*

*HAWAII
(U.S.A.)*

*NORTHERN
MARIANA ISLANDS
(U.S.A.)*

**MARSHALL
ISLANDS**

*Johnston Atoll
(U.S.A.)*

*REVILLA GIGEDO
ISLANDS
(MEXICO)*

Guam (U.S.A.)

MICRONESIA

PALAU

**FED. STATES
OF MICRONESIA**

*GILBERT
ISLANDS*

Kiritimati

*PACIFIC
OCEAN*

*Clipperton Island
(FRANCE)*

**PAPUA
NEW
GUINEA**

NAURU

**SOLOMON
ISLANDS**

MELANESIA

K I R I B A T I

TUVALU

Tokelau

MARQUESAS ISLANDS

*GALÁPAGOS
ISLANDS
(ECUADOR)*

SOUTH AMERICA

*CORAL
SEA*

VANUATU

FIJI

4   3   1

*COOK
ISLANDS
(N.Z.)*

2

TONGA

*French Polynesia
(FRANCE)*

Tahiti

*TUBUAI
ISLANDS*

*TUAMOTU
ISLANDS*

*Pitcairn Island
(U.K.)*

*Easter Island
(CHILE)*

*San Félix
(CHILE)*

AUSTRALIA

*New Caledonia
(FRANCE)*

*Norfolk Island
(AUSTRALIA)*

*JUAN FERNÁNDEZ
ISLANDS
(CHILE)*

O C E A N I A

**NEW
ZEALAND**

*CHATHAM ISLANDS
(N.Z.)*

*TASMAN
SEA*

Stewart Island

*AUCKLAND
ISLANDS
(N.Z.)*

*Campbell Island
(N.Z.)*

KEY
1 *American Samoa* (U.S.A.)
2 *Niue* (New Zealand)
3 **SAMOA**
4 *WALLIS & FUTUNA* (FRANCE)

See page 181 for a larger scale map

0   1,000 miles

0   1,500 km

N
W   E
S

Arctic Ocean
and Islands

The center of the Arctic Ocean is frozen all year round. This is the location of the North Pole. The surrounding waters only freeze over in winter. The Arctic coasts of North America, Europe, and Asia include mountains, islands, and frozen plains, or tundra. Wildlife thrives around the Arctic Ocean. Peoples of the coasts and tundra live in small, remote communities, hunting seals and polar bears. There are also some bases for mining and oil production.

▶ *Polar bears' skin is black, to absorb heat from the sun.*

⭐ North Pole

Unlike the South Pole, which consists completely of land, the North Pole is a region made from drifting pack ice. The American explorer Robert Peary claimed to have led the first expedition that reached the North Pole, in 1909.

DISCOVER MORE

Greenland is 840,000 sq mi (2,175,600 sq km) in area and is considered to be the world's largest island. It is nearly one-quarter the size of the United States.

🔍 SEARCH AND FIND

Arctic Ocean

1   2   3   4   5   6   7

A
B
C
D
E
F
G
H
I
J

Alaska (U.S.A.)

Prudhoe Bay

Barrow

Point Barrow

CHUKCHI SEA

EAST SIBERIAN SEA

BEAUFORT SEA

Cape Bathurst

NEW SIBERIAN ISLANDS

Banks Island

M'Clure Strait

LAPTEV SEA

Victoria Island

Melville Island

North Magnetic Pole

ARCTIC OCEAN

CANADA

Prince of Wales Island

Severnaya Zemlya

RUSSIAN FEDERATION

North Pole

Ellesmere Island

LINCOLN SEA

Franz Josef Land

Foxe Basin

Baffin Island

Baffin Bay

KARA SEA

Amderma

Novaya Zemlya

Longyearbyen

Svalbard (NORWAY)

Average permanent extent of sea ice

Davis Strait

Greenland (DENMARK)

GREENLAND SEA

BARENTS SEA

Nuuk

North Cape

Murmansk

Denmark Strait

NORWEGIAN SEA

NORWAY

SWEDEN

FINLAND

ICELAND

Arctic Circle

0   200 miles

0   300 km

27

North America

North America lies between the Atlantic and Pacific oceans.
Its northern coastlines fringe the icy Arctic Ocean. Here the land is made up of mountains and windswept, treeless plains, known as tundra. A broad belt of forest crosses Canada from east to west. Across the US-Canadian border are the prairies, natural grasslands which are now mostly farmed. The southeast of the continent is hot and humid, while the southwest is very dry. Rugged mountain chains run from the Arctic to tropical Central America.

◄ *The landscape in Monument Valley, in Utah, is caused by the erosion of rocks.*

DISCOVER MORE

Lake Superior, between Canada and the United States, is the largest body of fresh water in the world. About 200 rivers drain into the lake, and it covers an area of 32,483 sq mi (84,131 sq km).

SEARCH AND FIND

Antigua & Barbuda .G7	Haiti G6
Bahamas G6	Honduras H5
Barbados G7	Jamaica G6
Belize G5	Mexico G4
Canada E4	Nicaragua H5
Costa Rica H5	Panama H6
Cuba G6	St. Kitts-Nevis G7
Dominica G7	St. Lucia G7
Dominican	St. Vincent & the
Republic G6	Grenadines G7
El Salvador H5	Trinidad & Tobago. .G7
Grenada G7	U.S.A. F4
Guatemala H5	

NORTH AMERICA FACTS

Area sq mi (sq km)	% of Earth's area	Population	Largest country by area sq mi (sq km)	Largest country by population
9,400,000 (24,346,000)	16.2	482,992,000	Canada 3,851,800 (9,976,162)	U.S.A. 288,369,000

NORTH AMERICA

ARCTIC
OCEAN

Greenland
(DENMARK)

BEAUFORT
SEA

Baffin
Bay

Alaska
(U.S.A.)

LABRADOR
SEA

Gulf of
Alaska

Hudson
Bay

C A N A D A

PACIFIC
OCEAN

ATLANTIC
OCEAN

U N I T E D   S T A T E S
O F   A M E R I C A

Bermuda
(U.K.)

Gulf of California

Gulf of
Mexico

BAHAMAS

CUBA

DOMINICAN
REPUBLIC

HAITI

MEXICO

JAMAICA

CARIBBEAN
SEA

1
5
3
6
7
4
2
8

GUATEMALA BELIZE
EL SALVADOR HONDURAS
NICARAGUA
COSTA RICA PANAMA

KEY
1 ANTIGUA & BARBUDA
2 BARBADOS
3 DOMINICA
4 GRENADA
5 ST. KITTS-NEVIS
6 ST. LUCIA
7 ST. VINCENT & THE GRENADINES
8 TRINIDAD & TOBAGO

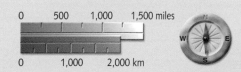

0   500   1,000   1,500 miles

0   1,000   2,000 km

N
W   E
S

Alaska

United States

Hawaii

United States of America

The United States of America lies between the Pacific and Atlantic oceans, bordering Canada to the north and Mexico to the south. To the west of the Rocky Mountains are salt flats, canyons, deserts, and coastal cities. To the east are prairie farms and the industrial cities of the Great Lakes and the Midwest. Beyond the Appalachian Mountains are East Coast cities and seaports. Alaska occupies the Arctic northwest, while Hawaii is made up of Pacific islands.

SEARCH AND FIND

U.S.A.			
★Washington, D.C..	C4	Missouri	E5
Alabama	D6	Montana	F4
Alaska	G2	Nebraska	F4
Arizona	G5	Nevada	H4
Arkansas	E5	New Hampshire	B4
California	H5	New Jersey	B4
Colorado	F5	New Mexico	F5
Connecticut	B4	New York	C4
Delaware	B4	North Carolina	C5
Florida	C6	North Dakota	F3
Georgia	C6	Ohio	D5
Hawaii	C2	Oklahoma	E5
Idaho	G4	Oregon	H4
Illinois	D5	Pennsylvania	C4
Indiana	D4	Rhode Island	B4
Iowa	E4	South Carolina	C5
Kansas	E5	South Dakota	F4
Kentucky	D5	Tennessee	D5
Louisiana	D6	Texas	E6
Maine	B3	Utah	G5
Maryland	C5	Vermont	C3
Massachusetts	B4	Virginia	C5
Michigan	D4	Washington	H3
Minnesota	E3	West Virginia	C5
Mississippi	D6	Wisconsin	E4
		Wyoming	G4

DISCOVER MORE

A road trip from one side of the United States to the other, traveling from the coast of New York to the coast of California, is around 3,000 mi (4,830 km).

COUNTRY FACTS

	Area sq mi (sq km)	Population	Language	Religion	Currency
U.S.A.	3,717,796 (9,629,092)	288,369,000	English	Catholic/Baptist	Dollar

UNITED STATES OF AMERICA

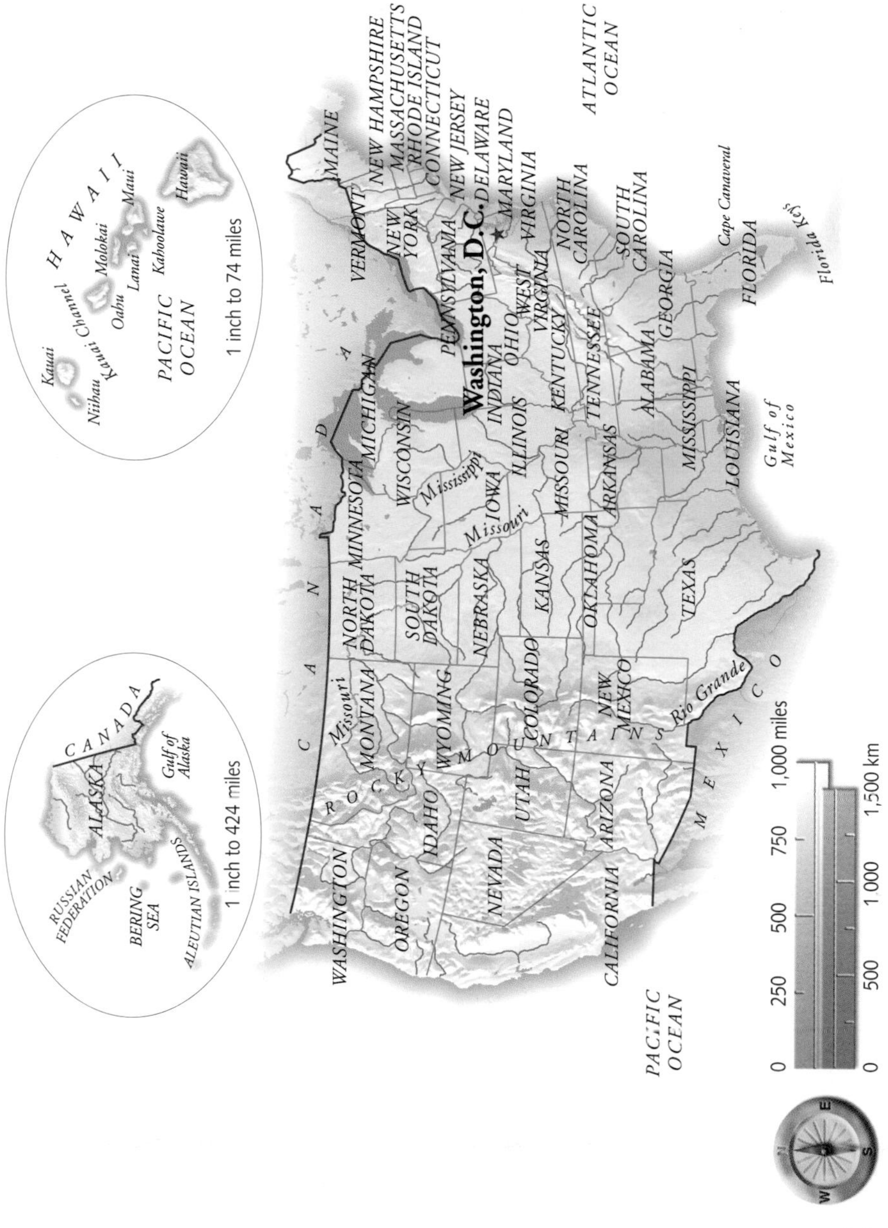

A
B
C
D
E
F
G
H
I
J

MAINE
NEW HAMPSHIRE
VERMONT
MASSACHUSETTS
RHODE ISLAND
CONNECTICUT
NEW YORK
NEW JERSEY
PENNSYLVANIA
DELAWARE
MARYLAND
Washington, D.C.
WEST VIRGINIA
VIRGINIA
NORTH CAROLINA
SOUTH CAROLINA
ATLANTIC OCEAN
Cape Canaveral
Florida Keys
FLORIDA
GEORGIA
ALABAMA
MISSISSIPPI
TENNESSEE
KENTUCKY
OHIO
INDIANA
ILLINOIS
MICHIGAN
WISCONSIN
Mississippi
Missouri
IOWA
MISSOURI
ARKANSAS
LOUISIANA
Gulf of Mexico
OKLAHOMA
KANSAS
NEBRASKA
SOUTH DAKOTA
NORTH DAKOTA
MINNESOTA
Missouri
MONTANA
WYOMING
COLORADO
NEW MEXICO
TEXAS
Rio Grande
M E X I C O
ROCKY MOUNTAINS
IDAHO
UTAH
ARIZONA
NEVADA
CALIFORNIA
OREGON
WASHINGTON
PACIFIC OCEAN
C A N A D A

HAWAII
Kauai
Niihau
Kauai Channel
Oahu
Molokai
Lanai
Maui
Kahoolawe
Hawaii
PACIFIC OCEAN
1 inch to 74 miles

CANADA
ALASKA
Gulf of Alaska
RUSSIAN FEDERATION
BERING SEA
ALEUTIAN ISLANDS
1 inch to 424 miles

1,000 miles
1,500 km
0 250 500 750
0 500 1,000

N E S W

U.S.A. *The Northeast*

The northeastern states stretch from the Great Lakes to the Atlantic Ocean and are crossed by hills, mountains, and farmland. New York City's skyscrapers look across the Hudson and East rivers. The green pastures of upstate New York are crossed by the Adirondack Mountains. The six other states of the region are Maine, New Hampshire, Vermont, Massachusetts, Rhode Island, and Connecticut. Collectively, they are known as New England.

DISCOVER MORE

Each day in the United States begins in the state of Maine. As the easternmost American state, it is always the first to see the sunrise, because the Sun rises in the east.

SEARCH AND FIND

New York
- Albany F4
Buffalo F2
New York City G4
Poughkeepsie F4
Rochester F2
Syracuse F3

Maine
- Augusta D5
Portland E5

Vermont
- Montpelier E4
Burlington E4

New Hampshire
- Concord E5
Manchester E5

Massachusetts
- Boston F5
Springfield F4
Worcester F5

Connecticut
- Hartford F4
Bridgeport G4
New Haven F4

Rhode Island
- Providence F5

STATE FACTS

	Area sq mi (sq km)	Population	Flower • Tree • Bird
New York	53,989 (139,832)	19,158,000	Rose • Sugar maple • Bluebird
Maine	33,741 (87,389)	1,294,000	White pinecone/tassel • Eastern white pine • Chickadee
Vermont	9,615 (24,903)	617,000	Red clover • Sugar maple • Hermit thrush
New Hampshire	9,283 (24,043)	1,275,000	Purple lilac • White birch • Purple finch
Massachusetts	9,241 (23,934)	6,428,000	Mayflower • American elm • Chickadee
Connecticut	5,544 (14,359)	3,461,000	Mountain laurel • White oak • Robin
Rhode Island	1,231 (3,188)	1,070,000	Violet • Red maple • Rhode Island red

NEW YORK • MAINE • VERMONT • NEW HAMPSHIRE
MASSACHUSETTS • CONNECTICUT • RHODE ISLAND

CANADA

MAINE

Mount Washington
6,288 ft
(1,917 m) ▲ • Augusta

VERMONT

Burlington

NEW HAMPSHIRE

Montpelier   • Portland

ATLANTIC OCEAN

NEW YORK

ADIRONDACK MTS

Hudson

Connecticut

Concord

• Manchester

Boston   Cape Cod

Lake Ontario

Albany   Worcester

MASSACHUSETTS

Syracuse

Springfield

Rochester

Hartford

Providence

RHODE ISLAND

Buffalo

Poughkeepsie

New Haven

CONNECTICUT

PENNSYLVANIA

NEW JERSEY

Bridgeport

Long Island

New York City

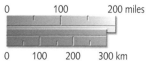

0   100   200 miles

0   100   200   300 km

Alaska

United States

Hawaii

U.S.A. *Mid-Atlantic*

The Atlantic coast runs south to Delaware and Maryland, broken by the inlets of Delaware Bay and Chesapeake Bay.

▲ In 1863, Fort Delaware was built on Pea Patch Island, in Delaware Bay.

The federal capital, Washington, is a large city on the Potomac River. Pennsylvania borders Lake Erie. It extends eastward across the Appalachian Mountains to the Delaware River. It contains the industrial city of Pittsburgh and historic Philadelphia. New Jersey is the most densely populated of all the states.

DISCOVER MORE

The Smithsonian Institution in Washington, D.C. is the world's biggest museum complex. It houses 14 museums and galleries and contains over 140 million items.

SEARCH AND FIND

Pennsylvania
- Harrisburg E4
- Allentown E5
- Erie D2
- Philadelphia E5
- Pittsburgh F3
- Scranton D5

Maryland
- Annapolis F5
- Baltimore F5

New Jersey
- Trenton E6
- Atlantic City F6
- Jersey City D6
- Newark D6
- Vineland E6

Delaware
- Dover F6

District of Columbia
- ★Washington F5

STATE FACTS

	Area sq mi (sq km)	Population	Flower • Tree • Bird
Pennsylvania	46,058 (119,290)	12,335,000	Mountain laurel • Hemlock • Ruffed grouse
Maryland	12,297 (31,849)	5,458,000	Black-eyed Susan • White oak • Baltimore oriole
New Jersey	8,215 (21,277)	8,590,000	Purple violet • Red oak • Eastern goldfinch
Delaware	2,396 (6,206)	807,000	Peach blossom • American holly • Blue hen chicken
District of Columbia	70 (181)	571,000	Western rhododendron • Western hemlock • Willow goldfinch

PENNSYLVANIA • MARYLAND • NEW JERSEY • DELAWARE
DISTRICT OF COLUMBIA

NEW YORK

Lake Erie

OHIO

Erie

PENNSYLVANIA

Scranton

Newark

Jersey City

Susquehanna

Delaware

Allentown

Trenton

Harrisburg

Philadelphia

NEW JERSEY

Pittsburgh

APPALACHIAN MOUNTAINS

Vineland

Atlantic City

Baltimore

Dover

Potomac

MARYLAND

Annapolis

Delaware Bay

DELAWARE

WEST VIRGINIA

Washington

★ D.C.

VIRGINIA

Chesapeake Bay

ATLANTIC OCEAN

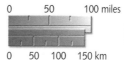

0   50   100 miles

0   50   100   150 km

Note: District of Columbia is a federal district, not a state

Alaska

United States

Hawaii

U.S.A. *The Deep South*

The American South borders the Gulf of Mexico. The climate is hot and humid, with hurricanes battering the coast in late summer and the fall. Farmers grow cotton and peanuts. The broad, muddy Mississippi River flows through the western part of the region before forming a broad delta on the Louisiana coast. The peninsula of Florida is popular with tourists.

▲ *The brown pelican lives along the coastline of North America and is Louisiana's state bird. It grows to 4 ft (1 m) long.*

DISCOVER MORE

Florida's Everglades form one of the world's biggest freshwater wetlands. They are home to alligators and venomous snakes such as the diamondback rattlesnake.

SEARCH AND FIND

Florida
- ■ Tallahassee F5
- Jacksonville F6
- Miami G6
- Orlando F6
- Tampa F5

Georgia
- ■ Atlanta E5
- Augusta E5

Arkansas
- ■ Little Rock E3

- Fayetteville D2

Alabama
- ■ Montgomery E4
- Birmingham E4
- Mobile F4

Louisiana
- ■ Baton Rouge F3
- New Orleans F3

Mississippi
- ■ Jackson E3
- Gulfport F4

STATE FACTS

	Area sq mi (sq km)	Population	Flower • Tree • Bird
Florida	59,928 (155,214)	16,713,000	Orange blossom • Sabal palmetto palm • Mockingbird
Georgia	58,977 (152,750)	8,560,000	Cherokee rose • Live oak • Brown thrasher
Arkansas	53,182 (137,741)	2,710,000	Apple blossom • Pine • Mockingbird
Alabama	52,237 (135,294)	4,487,000	Camellia • Southern longleaf pine • Yellowhammer
Louisiana	49,651 (128,596)	4,483,000	Magnolia • Cypress • Eastern brown pelican
Mississippi	48,286 (125,061)	2,872,000	Magnolia • Magnolia • Mockingbird

FLORIDA • GEORGIA • ARKANSAS
ALABAMA • LOUISIANA • MISSISSIPPI

MISSOURI

•Fayetteville

OKLAHOMA

ARKANSAS

Little
Rock

TEXAS

LOUISIANA

MISSISSIPPI

Jackson

Baton Rouge

New •
Orleans

Mississippi Delta

Red

Mississippi

TENNESSEE

Tennessee

Birmingham

ALABAMA

Montgomery

Alabama

Mobile•

•Gulfport

NORTH CAROLINA

Atlanta

Augusta

SOUTH CAROLINA

GEORGIA

Tallahassee

•Jacksonville

Orlando

FLORIDA

Tampa•

ATLANTIC OCEAN

Gulf of Mexico

•Miami

The Everglades

Florida Keys

0   100   200 miles

0   300 km

N W E S

U.S.A. *Appalachians*

Alaska

United States

Hawaii

The wooded slopes of the Appalachian Mountains—the second-largest range in America, after the Rockies—run through these southern states from northeast to southwest. The mountains are the oldest in North America and could have been formed up to 435 million years ago. The southern states are rich in coal. Tobacco and corn are grown on the region's fertile lowlands, and the green pastures of Kentucky are famous for their racehorses. The Atlantic Ocean coastline is made up of long sandy beaches, with many islands and lagoons.

DISCOVER MORE

Giant dunes and huge waves often occur off the North Carolina coast. This coastline has seen so many shipwrecks that it is known as "the Graveyard of the Atlantic."

SEARCH AND FIND

North Carolina
- Raleigh E5
- Charlotte E5
- Greensboro E5
- Winston-Salem E5

Virginia
- Richmond D5
- Norfolk D6

Tennessee
- Nashville E3
- Knoxville E4
- Memphis E2

Kentucky
- Frankfort D3
- Lexington D4
- Louisville D3

South Carolina
- Columbia E5
- Charleston F5
- Greenville E4
- Myrtle Beach E5

West Virginia
- Charleston D4
- Huntington D4

STATE FACTS

	Area sq mi (sq km)	Population	Flower • Tree • Bird
North Carolina	52,672 (136,420)	8,320,000	Dogwood • Pine • Cardinal
Virginia	42,326 (109,624)	7,294,000	Dogwood • Dogwood • Cardinal
Tennessee	42,146 (109,158)	5,797,000	Iris • Tulip poplar • Mockingbird
Kentucky	40,411 (104,664)	4,093,000	Goldenrod • Tulip poplar • Cardinal
South Carolina	31,189 (80,780)	4,107,000	Yellow jessamine • Palmetto • Carolina wren
West Virginia	24,231 (62,758)	1,802,000	Big rhododendron • Sugar maple • Cardinal

NORTH CAROLINA • VIRGINIA • TENNESSEE • KENTUCKY
SOUTH CAROLINA • WEST VIRGINIA

PENNSYLVANIA

OHIO

WEST VIRGINIA

MARYLAND

Charleston

Richmond

INDIANA

Frankfort Huntington

VIRGINIA • Norfolk

ILLINOIS

Louisville Lexington

Greensboro

KENTUCKY

Knoxville Winston-Salem Raleigh   Cape Hatteras

MISSOURI

Nashville

APPALACHIAN MOUNTAINS

NORTH CAROLINA

TENNESSEE

Charlotte

ARKANSAS

Memphis

Greenville   • Myrtle Beach

ATLANTIC OCEAN

MISSISSIPPI ALABAMA GEORGIA

Columbia

Savannah

SOUTH CAROLINA

Charleston

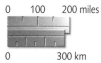

0   100   200 miles

0   300 km

N
W   E
S

Alaska

United States

Hawaii

U.S.A. *The Southwest*

The Southwest region of the United States borders the hot, dry lands of northern Mexico. Texas has modern cities such as Houston and Dallas. The state's wealth comes from its oil reserves and from cattle ranching on its hot, dusty plains. The farms of Oklahoma, to the north, produce wheat. Minerals are mined in mountainous New Mexico, and irrigation makes it possible to farm in Arizona, where there are large areas of hot desert.

◀ *Over hundreds of years, the 1,440 mi (2,320 km) long Colorado River in Arizona has eroded the rock to form islands.*

DISCOVER MORE

Texas is a huge state. It is the largest American state in size after Alaska. Its area is larger than the combined states of Illinois, Indiana, Iowa, Michigan, and Wisconsin.

SEARCH AND FIND

Texas
- Austin E6
- Amarillo D5
- Corpus Christi F6
- Dallas E6
- El Paso E3
- Houston F7
- McAllen G6
- San Antonio F6

New Mexico
- Santa Fe D4
- Albuquerque D4

Arizona
- Phoenix D2
- Tucson E2

Oklahoma
- Oklahoma City . .D6
- Tulsa D6

STATE FACTS

	Area sq mi (sq km)	Population	Flower • Tree • Bird
Texas	267,277 (692,247)	21,780,000	Bluebonnet • Pecan • Mockingbird
New Mexico	121,598 (314,939)	1,855,000	Yucca • Piñon • Roadrunner
Arizona	114,006 (295,276)	5,456,000	Saguaro cacti blossom • Paloverde • Cactus wren
Oklahoma	69,903 (181,049)	3,494,000	Mistletoe • Redbud • Scissor-tailed flycatcher

TEXAS • NEW MEXICO • ARIZONA • OKLAHOMA

NEVADA
UTAH
COLORADO
KANSAS
MISSOURI
CALIFORNIA
Grand Canyon
Colorado
ARIZONA
Phoenix
Gila
Tucson
Santa Fe
Albuquerque
Rio Grande
NEW MEXICO
El Paso
MEXICO
Rio Grande
Pecos
Amarillo
Oklahoma City
OKLAHOMA
Red
TEXAS
Dallas
Austin
Houston
San Antonio
Corpus Christi
McAllen
Gulf of Mexico
ARKANSAS
LOUISIANA
Tulsa

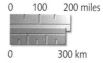

0   100   200 miles

0   300 km

Alaska

United States

Hawaii

U.S.A. *The Midwest*

The American Midwest lies between the Rocky Mountain states and the Mississippi River. These vast, flat prairies, or grasslands, are known as the Great Plains. They are crossed by the Missouri River. Most of the prairies are now farmed for wheat, corn, or soybeans. Patchworks of fields stretch as far as the eye can see. Cattle are raised in sparsely populated North and South Dakota. The state of Minnesota, which lies beside Lake Superior, has dairy farms and reserves of iron ore.

DISCOVER MORE

The United States can expect more than 900 tornadoes, or twisters, each year. Front-line states in "Tornado Alley" include Kansas, Nebraska, Iowa, and Missouri.

SEARCH AND FIND

Minnesota
- St. Paul D5
Duluth D5
Minneapolis D5
Kansas
- Topeka G4
Wichita G4
Nebraska
- Lincoln F4
Omaha F4
South Dakota
- Pierre E3

Sioux Falls E4
North Dakota
- Bismarck D3
Fargo D4
Missouri
- Jefferson City . . .G5
Kansas City F5
St. Louis G6
Iowa
- Des Moines F5
Cedar Rapids E5
Davenport E6

STATE FACTS

	Area sq mi (sq km)	Population	Flower • Tree • Bird
Minnesota	86,943 (225,182)	5,020,000	Pink and white lady's slipper • Red pine • Common loon
Kansas	82,282 (213,110)	2,716,000	Native sunflower • Cottonwood • Western meadowlark
Nebraska	77,358 (200,357)	1,729,000	Goldenrod • Cottonwood • Western meadowlark
South Dakota	77,121 (199,743)	761,000	Pasqueflower • Black Hills spruce • Chinese red-necked pheasant
North Dakota	70,704 (183,123)	634,000	Wild prairie rose • American elm • Western meadowlark
Missouri	69,709 (180,546)	5,673,000	Hawthorn • Dogwood • Bluebird
Iowa	56,276 (145,755)	2,937,000	Wild rose • Oak • Eastern goldfinch

MINNESOTA • KANSAS • NEBRASKA • SOUTH DAKOTA
NORTH DAKOTA • MISSOURI • IOWA

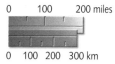

Alaska

United States

Hawaii

U.S.A. *Great Lakes*

The Great Lakes are fringed by dunes, bluffs, and forests. Wisconsin's green farmland provides pasture for cows, while wheat, soybeans, and corn are grown on the farmlands of Michigan, Illinois, Indiana, and Ohio. However, most people in this region are city dwellers. Detroit is the center of the US automobile industry. More than six million people live in the Chicago area.

◀ *Lake Michigan is the third largest of the Great Lakes— it is 22,400 sq mi (58,000 sq km) in area.*

DISCOVER MORE

Chicago's world-famous, 110-story Sears Tower stands at 1,450 ft (442 m) tall. Once the world's tallest skyscraper, it is still North America's tallest skyscraper.

SEARCH AND FIND

Michigan
- Lansing E5
Detroit E5
Flint E5
Grand Rapids E4
Wisconsin
- Madison E3
Milwaukee E4
Illinois
- Springfield G3
Chicago F4

Peoria F3
Ohio
- Columbus F6
Akron F6
Cincinnati G5
Cleveland F6
Dayton F5
Indiana
- Indianapolis F5
Fort Wayne F5
South Bend F4

STATE FACTS

	Area sq mi (sq km)	Population	Flower • Tree • Bird
Michigan	96,705 (250,465)	10,050,000	Apple blossom • White pine • Robin
Wisconsin	65,499 (169,642)	5,441,000	Wood violet • Sugar maple • Robin
Illinois	57,918 (150,007)	12,601,000	Native violet • White oak • Cardinal
Ohio	44,828 (116,104)	11,421,000	Scarlet carnation • Buckeye • Cardinal
Indiana	36,420 (94,327)	6,159,000	Peony • Tulip poplar • Cardinal

MICHIGAN • WISCONSIN • ILLINOIS • OHIO • INDIANA

CANADA

Lake Superior

MICHIGAN

MINNESOTA

WISCONSIN

Lake Huron

Wisconsin

IOWA

Grand
Rapids

•Flint

Milwaukee

Lansing •Detroit

Madison

Lake Michigan

Lake Erie

PENNSYLVANIA

Chicago

Cleveland•Akron

Mississippi

Illinois

South Bend
Fort Wayne

OHIO

•Peoria

•Columbus

Indianapolis

•Dayton
Cincinnati•

Springfield

INDIANA

Ohio

WEST VIRGINIA

ILLINOIS

MISSOURI

KENTUCKY

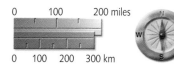

0   100   200 miles

0   100   200   300 km

Alaska

United States

Hawaii

U.S.A. *Mountain*

The Rocky Mountains form the backbone of the North American continent. Beneath blue skies, jagged peaks of granite streaked with snow descend to forests of pine and aspen. To the west, cattle are raised on the prairies of Montana and Wyoming. To the south, the peaks of Colorado attract skiers. To the east of the Rockies are the extraordinary landscapes of the Great Basin—salt flats, canyons, and deserts.

▲ *Colorado waterfalls can freeze in extremely low temperatures.*

DISCOVER MORE

The world's tallest active geyser is the Steamboat, in Yellowstone National Park, Wyoming. Steamboat can send up jets between 195 and 375 ft (60 to 115 m) high.

SEARCH AND FIND

Montana	Colorado Springs . .F6
■ Helena D4	***Wyoming***
Billings D5	■ Cheyenne E6
Nevada	Casper E5
■ Carson City F2	***Utah***
Las Vegas G3	■ Salt Lake City . . .E4
Reno E2	Ogden E4
Colorado	***Idaho***
■ Denver F6	■ Boise D3
Boulder F5	Idaho Falls D4

STATE FACTS

	Area sq mi (sq km)	Population	Flower • Tree • Bird
Montana	147,046 (380,849)	909,000	Bitterroot • Ponderosa pine • Western meadowlark
Nevada	110,567 (286,369)	2,173,000	Sagebrush • Single-leaf piñon/Bristle-cone pine • Mountain bluebird
Colorado	104,100 (269,619)	4,507,000	Rocky Mountain columbine • Colorado blue spruce • Lark bunting
Wyoming	97,818 (253,349)	499,000	Indian paintbrush • Plains cottonwood • Western meadowlark
Utah	84,904 (219,901)	2,316,000	Sego lily • Blue spruce • Seagull
Idaho	83,574 (216,457)	1,341,000	Syringa • White pine • Mountain bluebird

MONTANA • NEVADA • COLORADO • WYOMING • UTAH • IDAHO

CANADA

WASHINGTON

OREGON

BITTERROOT RANGE

R O C K Y

Snake

Helena

MONTANA

Yellowstone

NORTH DAKOTA

• Billings

IDAHO

• Boise

Idaho Falls

Yellowstone National Park

BIGHORN MOUNTAINS

SOUTH DAKOTA

Snake

WYOMING

M O U N T A I N S

Great Salt Lake

Reno
• Carson City

GREAT BASIN

Ogden

Salt Lake City

• Casper

Cheyenne

NEBRASKA

Lake Tahoe

NEVADA

UTAH

Boulder

• Denver
  Colorado
  Springs

KANSAS

CALIFORNIA

Colorado

Arkansas

Las Vegas

ARIZONA

COLORADO

NEW MEXICO

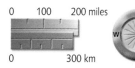

0   100   200 miles

0   300 km

U.S.A. *West Coast*

South of the seaport of Seattle, Washington, is a land of misty forests and volcanic mountain peaks. The Cascade Range runs southward into Oregon, with heavy rainfall on western slopes.

California is cool in the north and hot in the south. Its cities include beautiful San Francisco and sprawling Los Angeles—a world center of the entertainment and movie industry. Fruits are grown on the irrigated valleys between the Sierra Nevada and the Coast mountain ranges.

DISCOVER MORE

The highest temperature ever recorded in the United States was 134°F (57°C). This was measured in Death Valley in the state of California on July 10, 1913.

▼ *The Space Needle in Seattle, Washington, is 605 ft (184 m) high.*

SEARCH AND FIND

California	San Jose F3
■ Sacramento F3	*Oregon*
Bakersfield G3	■ Salem C3
Fresno G3	Eugene D3
Los Angeles H3	Portland C3
Oxnard H3	*Washington*
Riverside H4	■ Olympia B3
San Diego H4	Seattle B3
San Francisco F2	Spokane B5

STATE FACTS

	Area sq mi (sq km)	Population	Flower • Tree • Bird
California	158,869 (411,471)	35,116,000	Golden poppy • California redwood • California valley quail
Oregon	97,132 (251,572)	3,522,000	Oregon grape • Douglas fir • Western meadowlark
Washington	70,637 (182,949)	6,069,000	Western rhododendron • Western hemlock • Willow goldfinch

CALIFORNIA • OREGON • WASHINGTON

CANADA

WASHINGTON

Olympia • Seattle

Spokane •

Mount St. Helens
8,364 ft ▲
(2,549 m)

Snake

IDAHO

Portland •
Salem •

CASCADE RANGE

Eugene •

OREGON

Snake

COAST RANGES

Sacramento

Sacramento •

San Francisco •

San Jose •

SIERRA NEVADA

NEVADA

Fresno •

Mount Whitney ▲
14,449 ft
(4,118 m)

Death Valley

CALIFORNIA

Bakersfield •

Mojave Desert

Oxnard •
Los Angeles •

• Riverside

Colorado

ARIZONA

PACIFIC
OCEAN

• San Diego

MEXICO

0   100   200 miles

0   100   200   300 km

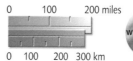

U.S.A. *Pacific States*

Alaska, the largest of the states, borders the Arctic and Pacific oceans. It lies just 56 mi (90 km) from the Russian Federation, in Asia. Alaska is a land of frozen tundra and icy mountains. Glaciers descend to foggy waters cruised by great whales. Industries include fishing and oil. The volcanic islands of Hawaii lie in the mid-Pacific Ocean. They have a warm climate and tropical vegetation. Crops include pineapples and sugarcane. Many tourists fly in from the mainland United States.

Astronomers carry out research at Hawaii's famous Mauna Kea observatory, at 13,760 ft (4,194 m) above sea level.

◀ *The Alaska Range in Denali National Park was formed millions of years ago by the Denali Fault.*

DISCOVER MORE

Mount Waialeale on Kauai Island, Hawaii, is one of the wettest places on Earth. This is because it has been known to experience 350 days of rain in one single year!

SEARCH AND FIND

Alaska			
■ Juneau	C7	Hilo	H6
Anchorage	C5	Kailua	F4
Fairbanks	B5	Kalaupapa	F5
Ketchikan	C7	Kaneohe	F4
Sitka	C7	Lanai City	G4
Hawaii		Lihue	F2
■ Honolulu	F4	Wailuku	G5
		Waipahu	F3

STATE FACTS

	Area sq mi (sq km)	Population	Flower • Tree • Bird
Alaska	615,230 (1,593,446)	644,000	Forget-me-not • Sitka spruce • Willow ptarmigan
Hawaii	6,459 (16,729)	1,245,000	Yellow hibiscus • Kukui (candlenut) • Hawaiian goose

ALASKA • HAWAII

A

0   250   500 miles

0   800 km

BROOKS RANGE

ALASKA

Bering Strait

Fairbanks

Yukon

B

CANADA

Mount McKinley
20,320 ft
(6,194 m)

ALASKA RANGE

Yukon

•Anchorage

C

Juneau
•Sitka

ALEXANDER ARCHIPELAGO

Ketchikan

Gulf of Alaska

Kodiak
Island

D

ALEUTIAN ISLANDS

Alaska Peninsula

Mount McKinley
North America's highest mountain
20,320 ft (6,194 m)

E

Kauai
Mount Kawaikini
5,243 ft ▲
(1,598 m)
•Lihue

Niihau

Oahu

F

Kaneohe
Waipahu• ■•Kailua
Honolulu Kalaupapa

Molokai

Wailuku

H   A
W
A
I   I

Lanai
City• Maui
Lanai

G

Mauna Kea
13,796 ft ▲
(4,205 m)

Hawaii

Hilo•

H

PACIFIC
OCEAN

▲
Mauna Loa
13,678 ft
(4,169 m)

I

0   50   100 miles

0   50   100   150 km

W ◆ E
S

J

51

Canada

Canada

Canada is the world's second-largest country, lying between the Pacific and Atlantic oceans. Its northern islands fringe the Arctic Ocean, and its southern regions extend to the prairies, the Great Lakes, and the St. Lawrence River. This vast area is home to only 30 million people. Most people choose to live in the far south because the northern forests and tundra have such severe winters.

◀ *Lake Louise is located in Banff National Park, part of the Rockies. Victoria Glacier forms part of the Rockies.*

DISCOVER MORE
Canada has two official languages: French and English. Around 69 per cent of Canadians speak mainly English and about 24 per cent speak mainly French.

SEARCH AND FIND

Canada	
★Ottawa D6	■ St. John's A5
■ Charlottetown . . .B5	■ Toronto D6
■ Edmonton G5	■ Victoria H6
■ Fredericton C6	■ Whitehorse H4
■ Halifax B6	■ Winnipeg F6
■ Iqaluit D3	■ Yellowknife G4
■ Quebec C6	Montreal C6
■ Regina F6	Vancouver H5

COUNTRY FACTS

	Area sq mi (sq km)	Population	Language	Religion	Currency
Canada	3,851,800 (9,976,162)	30,007,000	English/French	Catholic/Protestant	Dollar

CANADA

1 2 3 4 5 6 7

A B C D E F G H I J

St. John's

NEWFOUNDLAND AND LABRADOR

ATLANTIC OCEAN

PRINCE EDWARD ISLAND

Charlottetown

NEW BRUNSWICK NOVA SCOTIA

Halifax

Fredericton

LABRADOR SEA

QUEBEC

Quebec

Montreal Ottawa

Toronto

Lake Ontario

Iqaluit

Lake Erie

Greenland (DENMARK)

Lake Huron

NUNAVUT

ONTARIO

Lake Michigan

Lake Superior

Hudson Bay

CANADA

MANITOBA

UNITED STATES OF AMERICA

ARCTIC OCEAN

NORTHWEST TERRITORIES

Yellowknife

SASKATCHEWAN

Winnipeg

Regina

1,000 miles

ALBERTA

Edmonton

500

1,500 km

Mackenzie

ROCKY

BRITISH COLUMBIA

1,000

500

H

YUKON TERRITORY

Whitehorse

ALASKA (U.S.A.)

PACIFIC OCEAN

Vancouver Island

Vancouver

Victoria

0

N

E

W

S

53

Eastern Canada

Canada

This region lies to the east and south of Hudson Bay. It includes the Canadian Shield, which is a vast area of rock formations that were pitted and scarred by movements of ice in prehistoric times. These have filled with water to form thousands of lakes. The St. Lawrence River and the human-made St. Lawrence Seaway link the Great Lakes with the Atlantic Ocean and with coastal islands, such as Newfoundland. Major Canadian cities include English-speaking Toronto and French-speaking Montreal. Ottawa is Canada's national capital.

DISCOVER MORE

The Bay of Fundy, located between New Brunswick and Nova Scotia, experiences the highest tides in the world. The record stands at 54 ft (16.6 m).

SEARCH AND FIND

Quebec
- Quebec E5
Montreal E5
Sherbrooke E5
Ontario
★Ottawa F5
- Toronto F6
Hamilton F6
Kitchener G6
London G6
Windsor G6

Newfoundland and Labrador
- St. John's B3
New Brunswick
- Fredericton D5
Moncton D5
St. John D5
Nova Scotia
- Halifax D5
Prince Edward Island
- Charlottetown . . .D4

PROVINCE/TERRITORY FACTS

	Area sq mi (sq km)	Population	Flower
Quebec	594,860 (1,540,687)	7,237,000	White garden lily
Ontario	412,581 (1,068,585)	11,410,000	White trillium
Newfoundland and Labrador	156,649 (405,721)	513,000	Pitcher plant
New Brunswick	28,355 (73,439)	730,000	Violet
Nova Scotia	21,425 (55,490)	908,000	Trailing arbutus
Prince Edward Island	2,185 (5,659)	135,000	Lady's slipper

QUEBEC • ONTARIO • NEWFOUNDLAND AND LABRADOR
NEW BRUNSWICK • NOVA SCOTIA • PRINCE EDWARD ISLAND

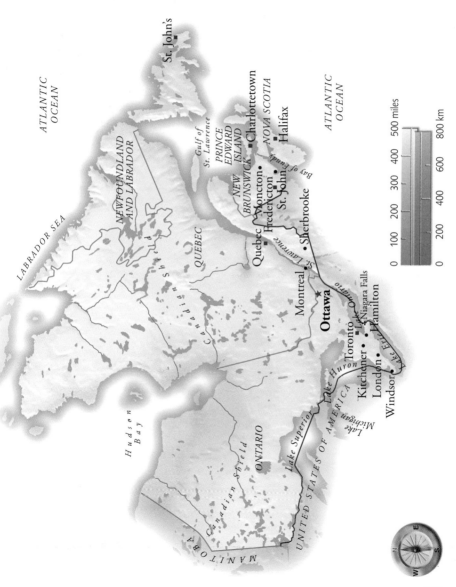

St. John's

ATLANTIC OCEAN

Charlottetown

NOVA SCOTIA

Halifax

ATLANTIC OCEAN

Gulf of St. Lawrence

PRINCE EDWARD ISLAND

NEWFOUNDLAND AND LABRADOR

Bay of Fundy

NEW BRUNSWICK

Moncton

Fredericton

St. John

LABRADOR SEA

Canadian Shield

QUEBEC

Quebec

Sherbrooke

St. Lawrence

Montreal

Ottawa

Ontario

Lake Ontario

Niagara Falls

Hamilton

Toronto

Kitchener

London

Windsor

Lake Erie

Lake Huron

Lake Michigan

Lake Superior

UNITED STATES OF AMERICA

Hudson Bay

Canadian Shield

ONTARIO

MANITOBA

500 miles
400
300
200
100
0

800 km
600
400
200
0

55

Canada

Northern and Western Canada

Canada's Prairie Provinces are Alberta, Saskatchewan, and Manitoba. Here, fields of wheat and cattle ranches stretch as far as the eye can see. Alberta has rich reserves of oil. The northern ranges of the Rocky Mountains run through Alberta and British Columbia, where the coastline forms a maze of islands. Canada's chief seaport on the Pacific coast is Vancouver. The territories of Canada's sparsely inhabited north include mountains, forests, lakes, and frozen tundra.

DISCOVER MORE

A pingo is a bump of soil on the Arctic tundra. It is pushed up by underground water. As the temperature rises, the ice melts. The pingo pops and collapses into a pond.

SEARCH AND FIND

Nunavut
- Iqaluit E7
Northwest Territories
- Yellowknife F3
British Columbia
- Victoria H2
Kamloops H2
Vancouver H2
Alberta
- Edmonton G3

Calgary H3
Lethbridge H3
Medicine Hat H3
Saskatchewan
- Regina H4
Saskatoon H4
Manitoba
- Winnipeg H5
Yukon Territory
- Whitehorse F2

PROVINCE/TERRITORY FACTS

	Area sq mi (sq km)	Population	Flower
Nunavut	818,959 (2,121,104)	27,000	Arctic poppy
Northwest Territories	503,951 (1,305,233)	37,000	Mountain avens
British Columbia	365,948 (947,805)	3,908,000	Pacific dogwood
Alberta	255,287 (661,193)	2,975,000	Wild rose
Saskatchewan	251,866 (652,333)	979,000	Prairie lily
Manitoba	250,947 (649,953)	1,120,000	Pasqueflower
Yukon Territory	186,661 (483,452)	29,000	Fireweed

NUNAVUT • NORTHWEST TERRITORIES • BRITISH COLUMBIA
ALBERTA • SASKATCHEWAN • MANITOBA • YUKON TERRITORY

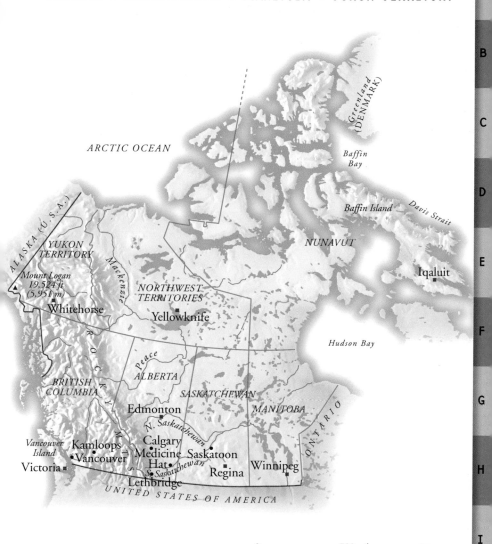

ARCTIC OCEAN

Greenland
(DENMARK)

Baffin
Bay

Baffin Island

Davis Strait

NUNAVUT

Iqaluit

ALASKA (U.S.A.)

YUKON
TERRITORY

Mackenzie

Mount Logan
19,524 ft
(5,951 m)

Whitehorse

NORTHWEST
TERRITORIES

Yellowknife

Hudson Bay

R O C K Y

Peace

ALBERTA

BRITISH
COLUMBIA

SASKATCHEWAN

MANITOBA

ONTARIO

Edmonton

N. Saskatchewan

Vancouver
Island

Kamloops

Vancouver

Victoria

Calgary

Medicine
Hat

S. Saskatchewan

Lethbridge

Saskatoon

Regina

Winnipeg

UNITED STATES OF AMERICA

0　　　　　　　　　500 miles

0　　　　500　　　1,000 km

N
W　　E
S

Mexico

South of the United States border, Mexico forms a large hook around the Bay of Campeche, ending in the humid forests of the Yucatán Peninsula. Mexico was the center of many ancient civilizations. Much of the country is made up of deserts and dusty plateaus, surrounded by the Sierra Madre Mountains in the east, west, and south. Mexico produces oil and textiles, and many of its factories are located in the vast sprawl of Mexico City.

◀ *Chichén Itzá was a major city built by the Mayans. The limestone temple at its center was dedicated to a serpent god, Quetzalcoatl.*

DISCOVER MORE

One of Mexico's most famous volcanoes is Popocatepetl, which rises to 17,930 ft (5,465 m). Despite its cone, shaped by intense heat, its upper slopes are covered in snow all year.

SEARCH AND FIND

Mexico		Mérida	C5
★Mexico City	E5	Mexicali	I2
Acapulco	E6	Monterrey	E4
Cancún	B5	Puebla	E5
Ciudad Juárez	G2	San Luis Potosí	E5
Guadalajara	F5	Tijuana	I2
León	E5	Torreón	F4

COUNTRY FACTS

	Area sq mi (sq km)	Population	Language	Religion	Currency
Mexico	756,066 (1,958,211)	97,483,000	Spanish	Catholic	Peso

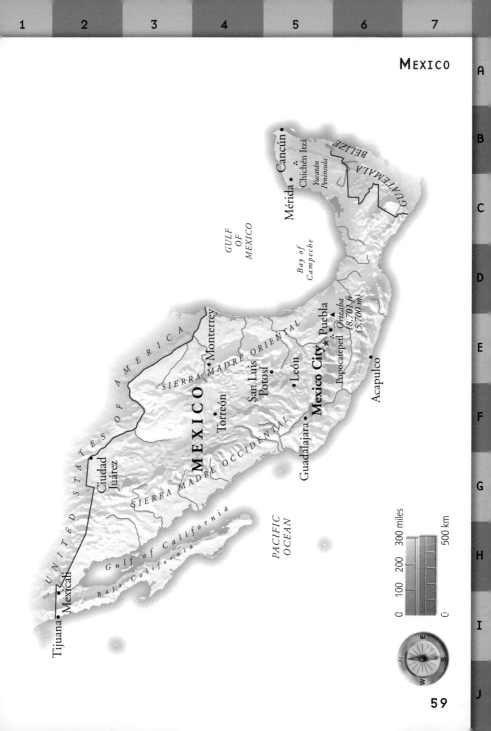

MEXICO

Guatemala
Belize
Honduras
El Salvador   Nicaragua
Costa Rica   Panama

Central America

A narrow bridge of land joining North and South America forms Central America. It is made up of seven nations that share rugged, volcanic mountainsides, forests, lakes, and steamy coastal plains. The hot, tropical climate is suitable for growing many crops, including bananas, sugarcane, and coffee. Northwestern coasts are at risk from hurricanes. The Panama Canal links the Pacific Ocean with the Atlantic Ocean through the Caribbean Sea. Spanish is Central America's most widely spoken language.

DISCOVER MORE

Two volcanic peaks rise from Lake Nicaragua's center—Ometepe Island. Once part of the Pacific, the lake may have been separated from the sea by volcanic activity.

SEARCH AND FIND

Nicaragua
★Managua F4
León F4
Honduras
★Tegucigalpa G3
San Pedro Sula ...G3
Guatemala
★Guatemala City ..H3
Quetzaltenango I3
Panama
★Panama City C5

David D6
Costa Rica
★San José E5
Limón E5
Puntarenas E5
Belize
★Belmopan G2
Belize City G2
El Salvador
★San Salvador ...H4
Santa Ana H4

COUNTRY FACTS

	Area sq mi (sq km)	Population	Language	Religion	Currency
Nicaragua	50,893 (131,813)	5,074,000	Spanish	Catholic	Córdoba
Honduras	43,278 (112,090)	6,480,000	Spanish	Catholic	Lempira
Guatemala	42,042 (108,889)	11,237,000	Spanish	Catholic	Quetzal
Panama	30,193 (78,200)	2,839,000	Spanish	Catholic	Balboa/US Dollar
Costa Rica	19,730 (51,101)	3,800,000	Spanish	Catholic	Colón
Belize	8,865 (22,960)	242,000	English/Creole	Catholic	Dollar
El Salvador	8,124 (21,041)	6,275,000	Spanish	Catholic	Colón

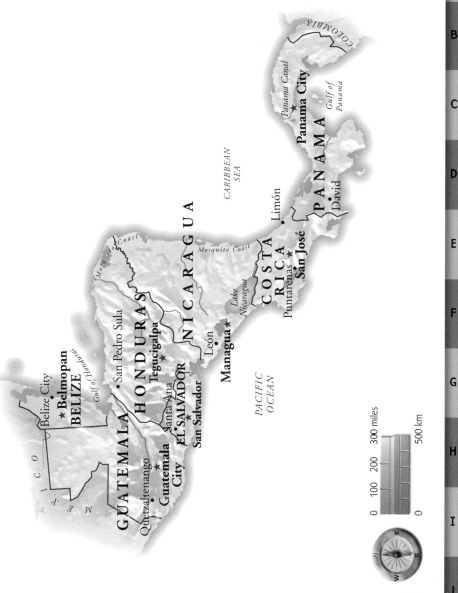

NICARAGUA • HONDURAS • GUATEMALA • PANAMA
COSTA RICA • BELIZE • EL SALVADOR

COLOMBIA

Panama Canal

Panama City

Gulf of
Panama

PANAMA

David

CARIBBEAN
SEA

Limón

San José

COSTA
RICA

Puntarenas

Mosquito Coast

Mosquito Coast

NICARAGUA

Lake
Nicaragua

León

Managua★

PACIFIC
OCEAN

San Pedro Sula

HONDURAS

Tegucigalpa ★

Gulf of Honduras

Belize City

Belmopan
★
BELIZE

Santa Ana

EL SALVADOR

San Salvador

C O

M E X I C O

GUATEMALA

Quetzaltenango

Guatemala
City ★

0 100 200 300 miles

0 500 km

N E S W

East Caribbean

The Bahamas and the Turks and Caicos are chains of low coral islands. South of these are the Greater Antilles, an island chain that forms the northern limits of the Caribbean Sea. The islands enjoy a warm, tropical climate. Crops include sugarcane, bananas, and coffee. The largest islands are Cuba, Jamaica, Puerto Rico, and Hispaniola, which is split between Haiti and the Dominican Republic.

◀ *The Bahamas is a cluster of more than 700 islands known for their shallow waters, but only 30 of them are inhabited.*

SEARCH AND FIND

Cuba
★Havana E2
Camagüey E3
Holguín E4
Santiago de Cuba . .F4
Dominican Republic
★Santo Domingo . .F5
Santiago E5

Haiti
★Port-au-Prince . . .F5
Cap Haïtien E5
Bahamas
★Nassau D3
Jamaica
★Kingston F4
Montego Bay F3

DISCOVER MORE
The fruits of the ackee tree are poisonous, but when they ripen, they contain creamy pulp which is safe. This is used to make Jamaica's national dish—saltfish and ackee.

COUNTRY FACTS

	Area sq mi (sq km)	Population	Language	Religion	Currency
Cuba	42,803 (110,860)	11,251,000	Spanish	NR*	Cuban Peso
Dominican Rep.	18,815 (48,731)	8,562,000	Spanish	Catholic	Peso
Haiti	10,714 (27,749)	7,820,000	Haitian Creole	Catholic/Voodoo	Gourde
Bahamas	5,382 (13,939)	302,000	English	Baptist/NR*/Catholic	Dollar
Jamaica	4,243 (10,989)	2,607,000	English	Pentecostal/NR/C**	Dollar

*Non-religious **Non-religious/Catholic

CUBA • DOMINICAN REPUBLIC • HAITI • BAHAMAS • JAMAICA

*ATLANTIC
OCEAN*

*Grand
Bahama*

BAHAMAS

Nassau
★

*TURKS AND
CAICOS ISLANDS*
(U.K.)

VIRGIN ISLANDS
(U.S.A. and U.K.)

Havana
★

C U B A Holguín • Cap Haïtien **DOMINICAN
REPUBLIC** **San Juan**
★
Camagüey • • Santiago *Puerto Rico*
(U.S.A.)

Isle of Youth

*CAYMAN
ISLANDS*
(U.K.)

Santiago **HAITI**
de Cuba **Port-au-** **Santo**
Prince **Domingo**
★

G R E A T E R   A N T I L L E S

Montego Bay ★
JAMAICA **Kingston**

C A R I B B E A N   S E A

0   100 200   300 miles

0   500 km

Lesser Antilles

West Caribbean

The Lesser Antilles form part of the loop of tropical islands that circle the Caribbean Sea. Many of the islands are volcanic. The northern section is known as the Leeward Islands. The section south from Dominica is known as the Windward Islands. Another section of the Lesser Antilles runs parallel to the coast of South America and includes Aruba, the remainder of the Netherlands Antilles, and Trinidad and Tobago. Trinidad, the largest island in the Lesser Antilles, has oil reserves.

SEARCH AND FIND

Trinidad and Tobago
★Port of Spain F5
Dominica
★Roseau D5
St. Lucia
★Castries E5
Antigua and Barbuda
★St. John's D5

Barbados
★Bridgetown E6
St. Vin. and the Gren.
★Kingstown E5
Grenada
★St. George's E5
St. Kitts-Nevis
★Basseterre D5

DISCOVER MORE
Trinidad's Pitch Lake contains hot, sticky, black tar, which covers about 140 acres (57 ha), and reaches a depth of 135 ft (41 m). It is even possible to walk across it.

COUNTRY FACTS

	Area sq mi (sq km)	Population	Language	Religion	Currency
Trinidad & Tobago	1,981 (5,131)	1,262,000	English	Catholic/Hindu	Dollar
Dominica	290 (751)	71,000	FC*/English	Catholic	EC Dollar**
St. Lucia	239 (619)	163,000	English/FC*	Catholic	EC Dollar**
Antigua & Barbuda	170 (440)	70,000	English	Anglican	EC Dollar**
Barbados	166 (430)	269,000	English	Anglican/Pentecostal	Dollar
St. Vin. & the Gren.	150 (389)	112,000	English	Non-religious/Anglican	EC Dollar**
Grenada	131 (339)	101,000	English	Catholic	EC Dollar**
St. Kitts-Nevis	104 (269)	46,000	English	Anglican/Methodist	EC Dollar**

*French Creole **East Caribbean Dollar

TRINIDAD AND TOBAGO • DOMINICA • ST. LUCIA
ANTIGUA AND BARBUDA • BARBADOS
ST. VINCENT AND THE GRENADINES
GRENADA • ST. KITTS-NEVIS

ANTIGUA AND
BARBUDA
Basseterre ★ ★ **St. John's**
ST. KITTS-NEVIS
Montserrat
(U.K.)
Guadeloupe (FRANCE)
Roseau ★ **DOMINICA**
Castries *Martinique* (FRANCE)
ST. LUCIA ★ ★ **BARBADOS**
ST. VINCENT AND ★ ★ **Bridgetown**
THE GRENADINES **Kingstown**
St. George's ★ **GRENADA**
Tobago
Aruba **Netherlands** **Port of Spain** ★ **TRINIDAD**
(NETHERLANDS) **Antilles** **AND TOBAGO**
Curaçao Bonaire *Trinidad*
V E N E Z U E L A

0   100   200   300 miles

0   500 km

South America

A narrow strip of land, called the Isthmus of Panama, acts as a bridge between North and South America. South America is the fourth-largest continent. Its northern regions are warm and tropical, while its far south stretches toward Antarctica, through cold, stormy seas. The Andes Mountains run like a rocky spine down the western side of the continent. Eastward are the great rain forests of the Amazon River basin, the grasslands of the Pampas, and the bleak valleys of Patagonia. South America contains the fewest countries of all the continents.

▶ *Sugar Loaf Mountain rises 1,325 ft (404 m) above Rio de Janeiro in Brazil, which lies on Guanabara Bay, on the Atlantic.*

DISCOVER MORE
The Amazon River is believed to contain 20 per cent of all the fresh water on Earth. The rain forest surrounding it is the world's richest habitat for wildlife and plants.

SEARCH AND FIND

Argentina	.......F3	Guyana	.........C4
Bolivia	.........E3	Paraguay	........E4
Brazil	.........D4	Peru	...........D3
Chile	.........E3	Suriname	......C4
Colombia	........C2	Uruguay	.........F4
Ecuador	.......C2	Venezuela	.......C3

SOUTH AMERICA FACTS

Area sq mi (sq km)	% of Earth's area	Population	Largest country by area sq mi (sq km)	Largest country by population
6,900,000 (17,871,000)	11.9	345,782,000	Brazil (8,511,957)	Brazil 176,871,126

*CARIBBEAN
SEA*

*Isthmus of
Panama*

VENEZUELA

GUYANA

SURINAME

*French Guiana
(FRANCE)*

COLOMBIA

ECUADOR

*Fernando de
Noronha Island*

*ATLANTIC
OCEAN*

B R A Z I L

P E R U

B O L I V I A

*PACIFIC
OCEAN*

CHILE

PARAGUAY

ARGENTINA

URUGUAY

*FALKLAND ISLANDS
(U.K.)*

SCOTIA SEA

0   500   1,000 miles

0   500   1,000 1,500 km

N
W   E
S

Colombia and Venezuela

At their northern limits, the Andes Mountains divide into three and run through Colombia, the easternmost range crossing into Venezuela. Below the mountains are fertile valleys and coastal plains, and tracts of rain forest in the south. In Venezuela, the Orinoco River flows through the Llanos grasslands to the Atlantic coast. Mineral wealth includes emeralds and Venezuelan oil. The biggest cities are Bogotá and Medellín in Colombia and Caracas in Venezuela.

▶ *La Candelaria is the oldest district in Bogotá. It contains colorful buildings.*

DISCOVER MORE

The world's highest waterfall is the Angel Falls, on the Carrao River in Venezuela. Its total drop is 3,212 ft (979 m), and its longest single section is 2,648 ft (807 m).

SEARCH AND FIND

Colombia		Venezuela	
★Bogotá	E3	★Caracas	C5
Barranquilla	C3	Barquisimeto	C4
Cali	E2	Ciudad Guayana	D6
Cartagena	C2	Maracaibo	C4
Medellín	D2	Valencia	C5

COUNTRY FACTS

	Area sq mi (sq km)	Population	Language	Religion	Currency
Colombia	440,762 (1,141,574)	44,531,000	Spanish	Catholic	Peso
Venezuela	352,143 (912,054)	23,054,000	Spanish	Catholic	Bolivar

COLOMBIA • VENEZUELA

CARIBBEAN SEA

LESSER ANTILLES

Barranquilla

Pico Cristóbal Colón ▲ *18,947 ft*
Cartagena• *(5,775 m)*

•Maracaibo

Caracas ★

Lake Maracaibo

•Valencia

Barquisimeto •

Orinoco

•Ciudad Guayana

Pico Bolívar 16,411 ft (5,001 m)

LLANOS

V E N E Z U E L A

GUYANA

Caroní

Angel Falls ★

PANAMA

Cordillera Occidental

ANDES MTS.

•Medellín

Magdalena

Cordillera Central

Cordillera Oriental

★ **Bogotá**

Cali •

C O L O M B I A

Orinoco

B R A Z I L

ECUADOR

PERU

Putumayo

0   100   200   300 miles

0   500 km

The Guianas

The Guiana Highlands run across the northeast of South America. They include the Pakaraima, Kanuku, Wilhelmina, and Oranje mountains, all of which are covered in rain forest. Rivers cross the plains on the Atlantic coast, where most people live. Many people grow sugarcane or rice, or mine bauxite, for making aluminum. The region is divided between independent Guyana and Suriname plus the smaller territory of French Guiana, which is a dependency of France.

▶ *Jaguars can be found in the forests and grasslands of Suriname. They often hide in shrubs and hunt at night.*

DISCOVER MORE
The Guianas are home to Native Americans, Chinese, Asian Indians, and Bengalis, as well as peoples of African descent, and peoples of mixed European descent.

SEARCH AND FIND

Guyana		Suriname	
★Georgetown	....C3	★Paramaribo	....D5
Linden	.........D3	Nieuw Nickerie	...D4

COUNTRY FACTS

	Area sq mi (sq km)	Population	Language	Religion	Currency
Guyana	83,000 (214,970)	749,000	English/Creole	Hindu/Protestant	Dollar
Suriname	63,039 (163,271)	417,000	Dutch/Sranan/Hindu	Hindu/Cath/SM*	S Guilder**

*Hindu/Catholic/Sunni Muslim   **Suriname Guilder

A

B

*ATLANTIC
OCEAN*

C

Georgetown

Nieuw
Nickerie

Linden

Paramaribo

D

VENEZUELA

PAKARAIMA MTS.

GUYANA

Brokopando Lake

*Mount Roraima
9,094 ft
(2,772 m)*

SURINAME

E

*WILHELMINA
MOUNTAINS*

Suriname

Maroni

French Guiana
(FRANCE)

*KANUKU
MOUNTAINS*

*Juliana Top
4,200 ft
(1,280 m)*

Essequibo

Courantyne

*ORANJE
MOUNTAINS*

F

B   R   A   Z   I   L

G

H

I

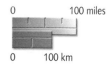

0   100 miles

0   100 km

J

Brazil

Brazil

Brazil is the largest and most populous country in all of South America. There are regions of mountain, dry scrub, and woodland, but much of Brazil's land is covered by tropical rain forest. A network of waterways flows through this dense vegetation into the Amazon River. This broad, muddy river flows eastward, eventually meeting the Atlantic Ocean. São Paulo and Rio de Janeiro, which are situated mostly on the coast, are both largely populated cities.

▲ *The statue* Christ the Redeemer *overlooks Rio de Janeiro.*

SEARCH AND FIND

Brazil	
★Brasília	.F5
Belém	.D5
Belo Horizonte	.G6
Curitiba	.H5
Fortaleza	.D7
Goiânia	.F5
Manaus	.D3
Porto Alegre	.H5
Recife	.E7
Rio de Janeiro	.G6
Salvador	.F7
Santos	.G5
São Paulo	.G5

DISCOVER MORE

In a good year Brazil can produce one-third of the world's coffee. The hot, humid climate and high altitudes are ideally suited to producing beans with intense aroma and flavor.

COUNTRY FACTS

	Area sq mi (sq km)	Population	Language	Religion	Currency
Brazil	3,286,470 (8,511,957)	176,871,000	Portuguese	Catholic	Real

BRAZIL

Amazon
South America's longest river
4,000 mi (6,437 km)

COLOMBIA

VENEZUELA

SURINAME

GUYANA

French Guiana (FRANCE)

Branco

GUYANA

Manaus

Amazon

Marajó Island

Belém

Fortaleza

S E L V A S

Madeira

Juruá

Purus

Xingu

Tocantins

SERTÃO

Recife

São Francisco

PERU

B R A Z I L

Sobradinho Reservoir

Salvador

MATO GROSSO PLATEAU

BRAZILIAN HIGHLANDS

BOLIVIA

Goiânia • **Brasília**

PARAGUAY

Paraná

Belo Horizonte

São Paulo

Santos

Rio de Janeiro

Itaipu Reservoir

Curitiba

ARGENTINA

ATLANTIC OCEAN

URUGUAY

Porto Alegre

Mirim Lake

0   100   200 miles

0   100   200   300 km

N
W   E
S

73

Peru and Ecuador

Ecuador and Peru occupy the central part of the Andes mountain range, which stretches for about 4,500 mi (7,200 km) down western South America. Mountain peoples herd llamas and grow potatoes and grain. Their ancestors developed civilizations in this region thousands of years ago. Western mountain slopes descend to the Pacific Ocean. Eastern gorges of the Andes drop to rain forests that surround the Amazon River.

◀ *People of the Bora community live in the Peruvian Amazon rain forest. They decorate themselves with feathers and body paint, and make their traditional dress out of bark cloth.*

SEARCH AND FIND

Peru	
★Lima F4	Piura D2
Arequipa H5	Trujillo E3
Callao F4	**Ecuador**
Chiclayo D3	★Quito B3
Cuzco G5	Cuenca C3
	Guayaquil C2

DISCOVER MORE
Ecuador takes its name from the equator, on which it lies. However, its capital, Quito, is located so high above the hot lowlands that the climate there is mild all year round.

COUNTRY FACTS

	Area sq mi (sq km)	Population	Language	Religion	Currency
Peru	496,223 (1,285,218)	25,662,000	Spanish	Catholic	New Sol
Ecuador	105,037 (272,046)	12,157,000	Spanish	Catholic	Dollar

A

B

C

D

E

F

G

H

I

J

COLOMBIA

★ **Quito**
Chimborazo
20,561 ft (6,267 m)

ECUADOR

Guayaquil •
Gulf of
Guayaquil

• Cuenca

Marañón

Amazon

Piura •

Chiclayo •

B R A Z I L

Ucayali

Trujillo •

Huascarán
22,205 ft
(6,768 m)

PERU

PACIFIC
OCEAN

A
N
D
E
S

M
O
U
N
T
A
I
N
S

Callao ★
Lima

Cuzco •

Lake
Titicaca

B
O
L
I
V
I
A

Arequipa •

CHILE

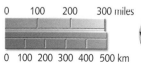

0   100   200   300 miles

0 100 200 300 400 500 km

75

Central South America

The Andes Mountains, which include a high plateau called the Altiplano, occupy the southwestern region of Bolivia. Lake Titicaca, on the Peruvian border, is 12,500 ft (3,810 m) above sea level and is the highest navigable lake in the world. Bolivia's lowlands are tropical, with rain forests and farmland used for cultivating bananas and sugarcane. The scrub-covered plain of the Gran Chaco extends into eastern Paraguay. Most Paraguayans live in the city of Asunción or on farms in the east.

DISCOVER MORE

The Itaipu Dam, situated on the Alto Paraná River, has the world's largest power plant. Its reservoir is larger than the world's two largest reservoirs combined.

◀ *Bolivian market traders are often female. Many wear traditional dresses and bowler hats.*

SEARCH AND FIND

Bolivia
★La Paz
  (Administrative) . . .D2
★Sucre
  (Legislative) E3
Cochabamba E3
Oruro E3

Potosi E3
Santa Cruz E4
Paraguay
★Asunción H6
Ciudad del Este . . .G7
Concepción G6
Encarnación H7

COUNTRY FACTS

	Area sq mi (sq km)	Population	Language	Religion	Currency
Bolivia	424,162 (1,098,580)	8,274,000	Spanish/Qucchua/Aymara	Catholic	Boliviano
Paraguay	157,046 (406,749)	5,206,000	Spanish/Guarani	Catholic	Guaraní

BOLIVIA • PARAGUAY

BRAZIL

PERU

Beni

Mamoré

BRAZIL

BOLIVIA

Lake
Titicaca

★ **La Paz**

Cochabamba

• Oruro

Santa
Cruz •

ALTIPLANO

★ **Sucre**

• Potosi

ANDES MOUNTAINS

GRAN
CHACO

CHILE

PARAGUAY

BRAZIL

ARGENTINA

Paraguay

• Concepción

Ciudad
del Este   Itaipu
Dam

★ **Asunción**

Paraguay

Alto Paraná

• Encarnación

0   100   200   300 miles

0   100 200 300 400 500 km

N
W   E
S

Southern Andes

The jagged ridges, volcanoes, and glaciers of the Andes Mountains continue southward through Chile and Argentina. The highest peak in the Americas is Chile's Cerro Aconcagua, at 22,310 ft (6,959 m). Chile's coast includes desert, valleys, and wild, rocky shores. Argentina's far north includes the scrub of the Gran Chaco. In the south, sheep graze the valleys of Patagonia. Cattle are raised on Argentina's grasslands and across the Rio de la Plata, in Uruguay.

DISCOVER MORE

The monkey puzzle tree, or Chile pine, can produce cones the size of a coconut. It grows in the southern Andes, often in bleak landscapes of volcanic ash and rocks.

▼ The massive Perito Moreno glacier on Lake Argentino, in Santa Cruz, has a surface area of 160 sq mi (257 sq km) and is 20 mi (30 km) long.

SEARCH AND FIND

Argentina		Chile	
★Buenos Aires	. . .E4	★Santiago	. . . . . . .E2
Córdoba	. . . . .D4	★Valparaiso	. . . . . .E2
La Plata	. . . . .E5	Antofagasta	. . . . . .C2
Mar del Plata	. . . . .E5	Concepción	. . . . . .E2
Mendoza	. . . . .D3	Temuco	. . . . .F2
Rosario	. . . . .D4	**Uruguay**	
San Miguel		★Montevideo	. . . . .E5
de Tucumán	. . . .C3	Salto	. . . . .D5

COUNTRY FACTS

	Area sq mi (sq km)	Population	Language	Religion	Currency
Argentina	1,057,518 (2,738,972)	36,260,00	Spanish	Catholic	Peso
Chile	292,258 (756,948)	15,116,000	Spanish	Catholic	Peso
Uruguay	68,039 (176,221)	3,360,000	Spanish	Catholic	Peso

ARGENTINA • CHILE • URUGUAY

Cerro Aconcagua
South America's highest mountain
22,310 ft (6,959 m)

PERU

ATACAMA DESERT

BOLIVIA

GRAN CHACO

PARAGUAY

Antofagasta

Ojos del Salado
22,575 ft
(6,880 m)

San Miguel
de Tucumán

Salado

Paraná

B R A Z I L

Cerro Aconcagua

Valparaíso

Santiago

Mendoza

Córdoba

Rosario

Salto

URUGUAY

PACIFIC
OCEAN

Concepción

Buenos Aires

Salado

PAMPAS La Plata

★ **Montevideo**

Río de la Plata

A R G E N T I N A

• Mar del Plata

CHILE

Temuco

Colorado

ATLANTIC
OCEAN

P A T A G O N I A

Chubut

Santa Cruz

FALKLAND ISLANDS
(U.K.)

Strait of Magellan

Tierra
del Fuego

Cape Horn

0 100 200 300 400 500 miles

0   500 km

N
W   E
S

79

Europe

The landmass of Eurasia is divided into two continents: Europe and Asia.
Europe is the smaller, westernmost part. Its coastline branches into
many peninsulas that form Scandinavia, Iberia, Italy, and the Balkans. Its
biggest islands are Great Britain, Ireland, and Iceland. Europe's border with
Asia runs along the Ural and Caucasus mountains. Its far north borders
the Arctic Ocean, and its southern coasts are on the Mediterranean Sea.

▼ *The Vltava River runs through
Prague, capital of the Czech Republic.*

DISCOVER MORE

The European part
of the Russian Federation
has Europe's highest
mountain (Mount Elbrus),
its longest river (Volga River),
its biggest lake (Ladoga
Lake), and its biggest
city (Moscow).

SEARCH AND FIND

Albania G4	Lithuania E5
Andorra F2	Luxembourg F3
Austria F4	Macedonia G5
Belarus E5	Moldova F5
Belgium E3	Monaco F3
Bosnia-Herzegovina .F4	Netherlands E3
Bulgaria G5	Norway D4
Croatia F4	Poland E4
Czech Republic . . .F4	Portugal F2
Denmark E3	Romania F5
Estonia D5	Russian Federation .D5
Finland D5	San Marino F4
France F3	Serbia & Montenegro .G4
Germany E3	Slovakia F4
Greece G5	Slovenia F4
Hungary F4	Spain G2
Iceland C2	Sweden D4
Ireland, Republic of .E2	Switzerland F3
Italy G4	Ukraine F5
Latvia E5	United Kingdom . . .E3
Liechtenstein F3	Vatican City G4

EUROPE FACTS

Area sq mi (sq km)	% of Earth's area	Population	Largest country by area sq mi (sq km)	Largest country by population
4,015,000 (10,400,000)	6.6	692,592,000	Ukraine* 233,089 (603,700)	Germany* 82,440,000

*largest country entirely in Europe

Scandinavia

Europe's far north borders the frozen Arctic Circle. It includes the bleak moors of Iceland, and the lakes, forests, and mountains of the Scandinavian peninsula and Finland. Deep-sea inlets known as fjords border the North Sea. Norway and Sweden stretch southward toward the small country of Denmark, whose lush, green farmland occupies the Jutland peninsula and its nearby islands.

▲ *Copenhagen is Denmark's largest city.*

SEARCH AND FIND

Sweden		Norway	
★Stockholm	....F4	★Oslo	.........F3
Göteborg	........G3	Bergen	.........F2
Malmö	.......H3	Stavanger	......F2
Uppsala	........F4	**Iceland**	
Västerås	.......F4	★Reykjavik	......C2
Finland		**Denmark**	
★Helsinki	......F6	★Copenhagen	....H3
Tampere	.......F5	Århus	.........H3
Turku	.........F5	Odense	........H3

DISCOVER MORE

Iceland is one of the world's most well-known volcanic hot spots. Hot water from deep underground is used to heat most of the island's homes and greenhouses.

COUNTRY FACTS

	Area sq mi (sq km)	Population	Language	Religion	Currency
Sweden	173,731 (449,963)	8,940,000	Swedish	Evangelical/Lutheran	Krona
Finland	130,127 (337,029)	5,206,000	Finnish	Evangelical/Lutheran	Euro
Norway	125,181 (324,219)	4,552,000	Norwegian	Evangelical/Lutheran	Krone
Iceland	39,699 (102,819)	288,000	Icelandic	Evangelical/Lutheran	Krona
Denmark	16,639 (43,095)	5,293,000	Danish	Evangelical/Lutheran	Krone

SWEDEN • FINLAND • NORWAY • ICELAND • DENMARK

A

B

ARCTIC OCEAN

North Cape

ICELAND

Reykjavik ★

1 inch to 69 miles

C

LAPLAND

RUSSIAN FEDERATION

D

ATLANTIC
OCEAN

FINLAND

E

Gulf of Bothnia

NORWAY   SWEDEN

Tampere
•

Åland
Island
(FINLAND)

Turku
•

★ Helsinki

F

Bergen
•

Oslo ★

• Stavanger

Uppsala
•

Västerås
•

Stockholm
★

NORTH SEA

Lake
Vänern

BALTIC SEA

G

• Göteborg

Århus
•

Copenhagen
★ ★

Bornholm
(DENMARK)

H

DENMARK

Odense
•

Malmö
•

GERMANY

I

J

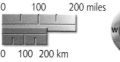

0   100   200 miles

0   100 200 km

United
Kingdom

Republic
of Ireland

British Isles

The British Isles lie in shallow waters off northwestern Europe. Thanks to warm ocean currents, they enjoy a generally mild, moist climate. They have green fields, moors, and highlands, as well as large, crowded cities. The two largest islands are called Great Britain and Ireland. The United Kingdom brings together the countries of England, Scotland, Wales, and Northern Ireland. The Republic of Ireland is independent.

DISCOVER MORE
The Irish people descend mainly from Celtic tribes that settled in Ireland over 2,000 years ago. The Irish encourage the use of the ancient Celtic language, Gaelic.

▼ *London's Tower Bridge, built across the Thames River in 1894, was once the largest bascule (seesaw) bridge.*

SEARCH AND FIND

United Kingdom
★London G5
■ Belfast E3
■ Cardiff G4
■ Edinburgh D4
Birmingham G5
Bristol G4
Glasgow D4
Leeds F5

Liverpool F4
Manchester F4
Newcastle upon
   Tyne E5
Nottingham F5
Sheffield F5
Republic of Ireland
★Dublin F3
Cork G2

COUNTRY FACTS

	Area sq mi (sq km)	Population	Language	Religion	Currency
United Kingdom	94,525 (244,820)	58,789,000	English	Anglican	Pound
Republic of Ireland	27,135 (70,280)	3,917,000	English	Catholic	Euro

United Kingdom • Republic of Ireland

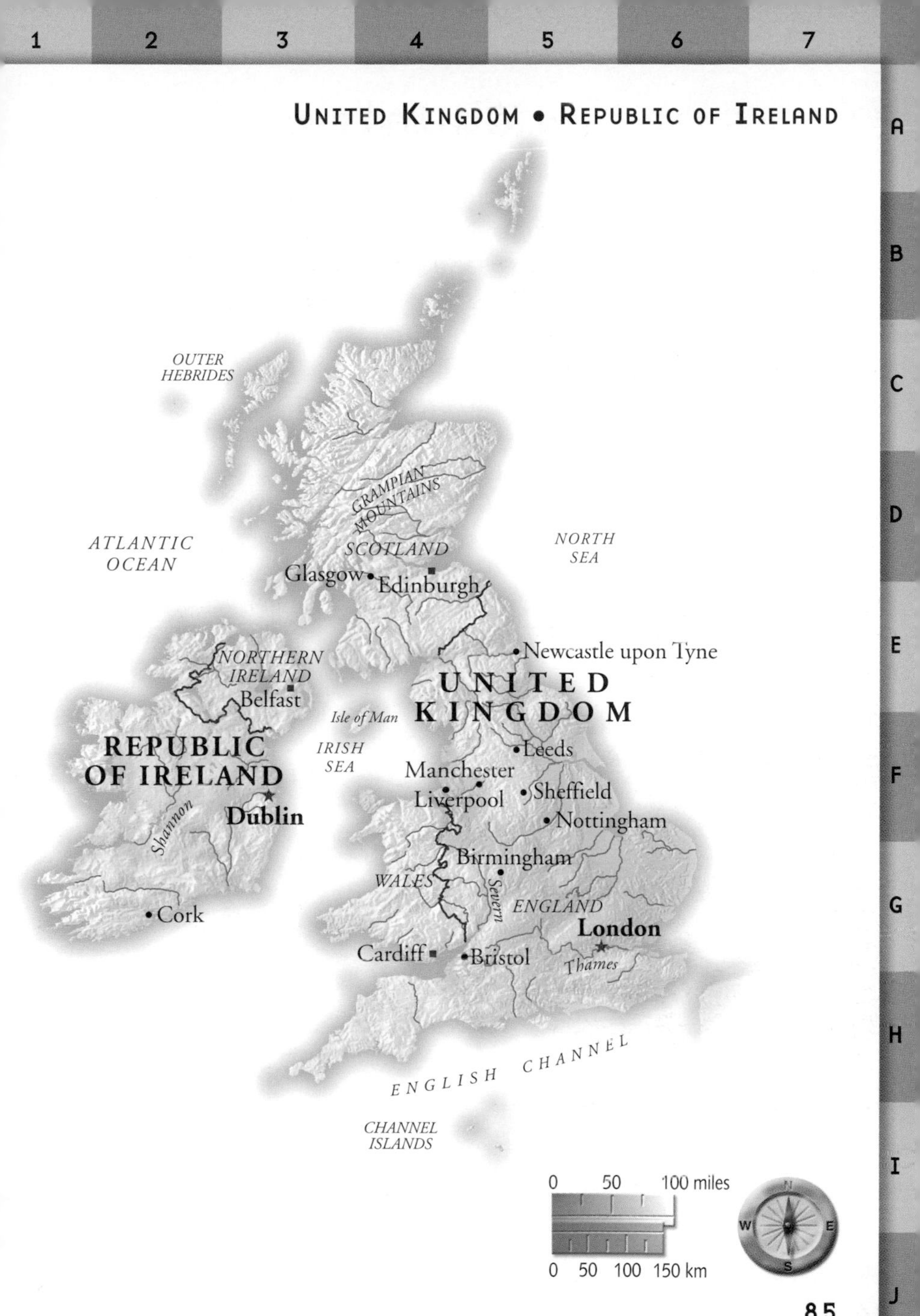

1
2
3
4
5
6
7
A
B
C
D
E
F
G
H
I
J
OUTER HEBRIDES
ATLANTIC OCEAN
GRAMPIAN MOUNTAINS
SCOTLAND
NORTH SEA
Glasgow
Edinburgh
NORTHERN IRELAND
Belfast
Newcastle upon Tyne
UNITED KINGDOM
Isle of Man
IRISH SEA
REPUBLIC OF IRELAND
Dublin
Shannon
Leeds
Manchester
Liverpool
Sheffield
Nottingham
Birmingham
WALES
Severn
ENGLAND
Cork
London
Cardiff
Bristol
Thames
ENGLISH CHANNEL
CHANNEL ISLANDS
0 50 100 miles
0 50 100 150 km
N
W
E
S

Low Countries

Netherlands

Belgium

Luxembourg

Between France and Germany, the North Sea coast is low-lying, flat, and divided by great rivers. New land has been artificially created by sealing off coastal waters and draining away the sea. Belgium and the Netherlands have beautiful old towns as well as modern cities, such as the great seaport of Rotterdam. Inland, flat farmland rises to the wooded hills of Belgium's Ardennes region and the tiny country of Luxembourg.

◀ *Windmills power pumps used to drain flooded fields throughout the Netherlands.*

DISCOVER MORE

Belgians are divided into two major groups—Flemings and Walloons. Flemings live in northern Belgium and speak Flemish. Walloons live in southern Belgium and speak French.

SEARCH AND FIND

Netherlands		Belgium	
★Amsterdam	D4	★Brussels	F4
★The Hague	D4	Antwerp	F4
Arnhem	D5	Ghent	F3
Eindhoven	E5	Liège	G5
Rotterdam	E4	**Luxembourg**	
Utrecht	D4	★Luxembourg	H6

COUNTRY FACTS

	Area sq mi (sq km)	Population	Language	Religion	Currency
Netherlands	16,033 (41,525)	15,987,000	Dutch	Catholic	Euro
Bolgium	11,780 (30,510)	10,310,000	Flemish/French	Catholic	Euro
Luxembourg	999 (2,587)	440,000	French	Catholic	Euro

NETHERLANDS • BELGIUM • LUXEMBOURG

WEST FRISIAN ISLANDS

Lake Ijssel

NORTH SEA

NETHERLANDS

★ **Amsterdam**

The Hague ★

• Utrecht

• Arnhem

Lek

• Rotterdam

Waal

GERMANY

• Eindhoven

• Antwerp

Ghent •

★ **Brussels**

BELGIUM

Meuse

• Liège

ARDENNES

GERMANY

FRANCE

LUXEMBOURG

★ **Luxembourg**

0   50 miles

0   50 km

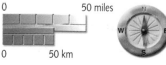

France
Monaco
Andorra

France and Its Neighbors

France lies at the heart of western Europe. It is located between the English Channel, the Atlantic Ocean, and the warm, blue Mediterranean Sea. France is a land of plains, crossed by rivers that drain the Massif Central highlands and the snowy peaks of the Pyrenees and Alps. France borders two independent states: Andorra and Monaco.

DISCOVER MORE

The Eiffel Tower is the best-known landmark in Paris. This iron needle, built by Eiffel in 1889, is 980 ft (300 m) high. From the top, 42 mi (67 km) of landscape can be seen.

◀ *Many varieties of lavender flourish throughout the southern Alpine region of France.*

SEARCH AND FIND

France		Nice	F6
★Paris	C4	Strasbourg	C6
Bordeaux	F3	Toulouse	F3
Lille	B4	**Andorra**	
Lyon	E5	★Andorra la Vella	G3
Marseille	G5	**Monaco**	
Nantes	D2	★Monaco	F6

COUNTRY FACTS

	Area sq mi (sq km)	Population	Language	Religion	Currency
France	211,208 (547,029)	59,080,000	French	Catholic	Euro
Andorra	181 (469)	66,000	Catalán	Catholic	Euro
Monaco	0.75 (1.95)	32,000	French	Catholic	Euro

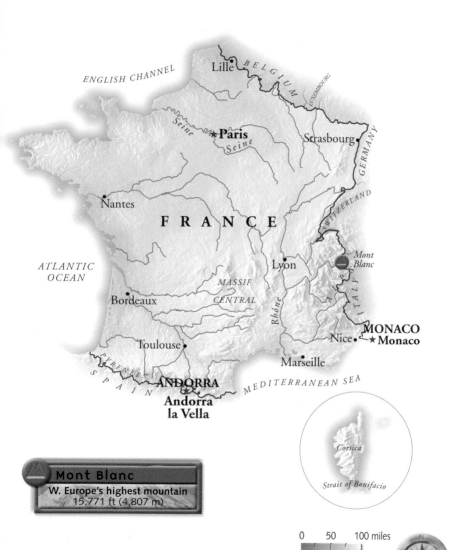

FRANCE • ANDORRA • MONACO

ENGLISH CHANNEL

Lille

BELGIUM

LUXEMBOURG

Seine

★ **Paris**

Seine

Strasbourg

GERMANY

Nantes

SWITZERLAND

F R A N C E

ATLANTIC OCEAN

Lyon

Mont Blanc

MASSIF CENTRAL

Bordeaux

Rhône

ITALY

Toulouse

MONACO
★ **Monaco**

Nice

PYRENEES

SPAIN

ANDORRA

Andorra la Vella

MEDITERRANEAN SEA

Marseille

Corsica

Strait of Bonifacio

Mont Blanc
W. Europe's highest mountain
15,771 ft (4,807 m)

0   50   100 miles

0   50   100 150 km

N
W   E
S

Portugal

Spain

Iberian Peninsula

The Iberian peninsula is a great slab of land extending into the Atlantic Ocean. Just 8 mi (13 km) from Africa, it forms the northern gateway to the Mediterranean Sea. The peninsula is occupied by two nations: Spain and Portugal. The central region occupies the Meseta, a hot, dusty plateau, which is surrounded by the high ranges of the Cantabrian Mountains, the Pyrenees, and the Sierra Nevada.

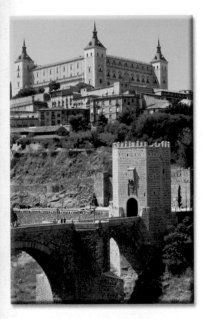

◀ *Toledo was the capital of Spain until 1560. Today, the city is still an important center of medieval history.*

DISCOVER MORE

More than one-third of the Iberian peninsula receives less than 20 in (500 mm) of rain each year. Large parts of the peninsula are at risk of becoming desert areas.

SEARCH AND FIND

Spain	Seville G3
★Madrid E4	Toledo E3
Barcelona D6	Valencia E5
Bilbao C4	**Portugal**
Málaga G3	★Lisbon F1
Murcia F5	Braga D2
Palma E7	Porto D1

COUNTRY FACTS

	Area sq mi (sq km)	Population	Language	Religion	Currency
Spain	195,364 (505,993)	40,847,000	Spanish	Catholic	Euro
Portugal	35,672 (92,390)	10,318,000	Portuguese	Catholic	Euro

SPANPORTUGAL

Bay of Biscay

CANTABRIAN MOUNTAINS

•Bilbao

F R A N C E

PYRENEES

ANDORRA

Ebro

Ebro

Barcelona•

ATLANTIC OCEAN

•Braga

•Pôrto

S P A I N

Madrid ★

PORTUGAL

•Toledo

•Palma

Valencia•

*BALEARIC
ISLANDS*

Tagus

★**Lisbon**

Murcia•

Costa Blanca

MEDITERRANEAN SEA

Seville•

SIERRA NEVADA

Málaga•

Costa del Sol

•Gibraltar (U.K.)

Strait of Gibraltar

0   100   200 miles

0   100 200 300 km

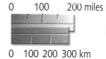

Germany

Germany

Germany, in western Europe, borders France and the Low Countries to the west, and Poland and the Czech Republic to the east. It stretches from the Bavarian Alps to the North and Baltic seas, and is a land of mountains, forests, heaths, and plains. These are crossed by some of Europe's most famous rivers, including the Rhine, Elbe, and Danube. Germany's old medieval towns contrast with large, modern cities, centers of industry and commerce.

▶ *Built around 900 B.C.E. the Rheinstein Castle rises above the mighty Rhine River in the Loreley Valley on a 270 ft (82 m) high rocky ridge.*

DISCOVER MORE
German factories are well known for producing some of the world's best-known makes of cars, such as Volkswagen, BMW, and Mercedes. These are exported worldwide.

SEARCH AND FIND

Germany		Frankfurt am Main. .F3
★Berlin D6		Hamburg C4
Bremen C3		Hannover D4
Cologne (Köln) E2		Mannheim F3
Dresden E6		Munich G5
Düsseldorf E2		Nuremberg F5
Essen E2		Stuttgart G4

COUNTRY FACTS

	Area sq mi (sq km)	Population	Language	Religion	Currency
Germany	137,803 (356,910)	82,440,000	German	Lutheran/Catholic	Euro

GERMANY

DENMARK

NORTH
SEA

BALTIC SEA

POLAND

Hamburg

Bremen

Elbe

•Hannover

Berlin
★

NETHERLANDS

Rhine

HARZ

Elbe

•Essen
•Düsseldorf
•Cologne (Köln)

GERMANY

Dresden•

BELGIUM

Rhine

CZECH REPUBLIC

LUXEMBOURG

•Frankfurt am Main

Main

•Mannheim

•Nuremberg

FRANCE

Rhine

BLACK FOREST

•Stuttgart

Danube

Munich•

SWITZERLAND

BAVARIAN ALPS

AUSTRIA

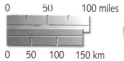

0   50   100 miles

0   50   100   150 km

N
W   E
S

93

The Alps

Austria, Switzerland, and the little state of Liechtenstein occupy western Europe's highest mountain range, the Alps. These divide the cool north from the sunny south, and are home to speakers of French, German, Italian, and Romansh. Beneath snow-covered peaks are rushing rivers and still lakes. Steep valleys, green and filled with wildflowers in summer, provide pasture for cattle. Industries include tourism, dairy produce, clock making, and timber.

DISCOVER MORE
Because of changes in climate in recent years, the Alps are becoming less snowy. This is likely to have an adverse effect on winter sports and the tourist trade in the region.

◀ *The Alps mountain range stretches for 660 mi (1,060 km) and crosses seven countries.*

SEARCH AND FIND

Austria		Switzerland	
★Vienna	C3	★Bern	I4
Graz	C4	Basel	I3
Innsbruck	F4	Geneva	J5
Klagenfurt	D4	Zürich	H4
Linz	D3	**Liechtenstein**	
Salzburg	E3	★Vaduz	G4

COUNTRY FACTS

	Area sq mi (sq km)	Population	Language	Religion	Currency
Austria	32,374 (83,849)	8,065,000	German	Catholic	Euro
Switzerland	15,942 (41,290)	7,318,000	German/French/Italian	Catholic/Protestant	Franc
Liechtenstein	62 (161)	34,000	German	Catholic	Swiss Franc

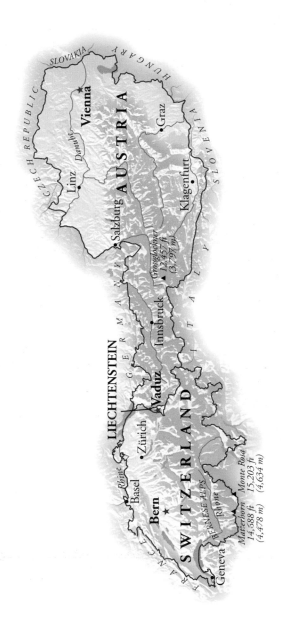

SLOVAKIA

HUNGARY

CZECH REPUBLIC

AUSTRIA

Vienna

Linz

Danube

Graz

SLOVENIA

Klagenfurt

Salzburg

Grossglockner
12,457 ft
(3,797 m)

G E R M A N Y

I T A L Y

LIECHTENSTEIN

Innsbruck

Vaduz

Zürich

SWITZERLAND

Rhine

Basel

Bern

BERNESE ALPS

Rhone

Matterhorn
14,588 ft
(4,478 m)

Monte Rosa
15,203 ft
(4,634 m)

FRANCE

Geneva

100 miles

50

0

150 km

100

50

0

Italy and Its Neighbors

The Italian peninsula stretches southward from the Alps. The Apennine mountain range forms a rocky backbone for most of its length. Most industrial regions are in the north. Italy has many beautiful historical cities. Its territory encloses tiny San Marino and the world's smallest independent state, called Vatican City. The island nation of Malta lies to the south of the volcanic island of Sicily.

DISCOVER MORE

Vatican City is located in the city of Rome. The state is ruled by the Pope who is head of the Catholic Church. Vatican City has a population of less than 1,000 people.

◀ *Boats called gondolas are used to transport people on Venice's waterways.*

SEARCH AND FIND

Italy
★Rome E4
Florence D4
Genoa C3
Milan C3
Naples E5
Palermo G5
Turin C2
Venice C4
Malta
★Valletta I5
San Marino
★San Marino D4
Vatican City E4

COUNTRY FACTS

	Area sq mi (sq km)	Population	Language	Religion	Currency
Italy	116,305 (301,230)	56,306,000	Italian	Catholic	Euro
Malta	124 (321)	378,000	Maltese/English	Catholic	Euro
San Marino	23 (60)	27,000	Italian	Catholic	Euro
Vatican City	0.17 (0.44)	860	Italian/Latin	Catholic	Euro

ITALY • MALTA • SAN MARINO • VATICAN CITY

AUSTRIA

SWITZERLAND   ALPS

SLOVENIA

FRANCE

Monte Rosa
15,203 ft
(4,634 m)

•Milan
•Venice

•Turin

Po

Genoa

SAN MARINO
★**San Marino**

A P E N N I N E S

Florence

LIGURIAN
SEA

I T A L Y

ADRIATIC SEA

Tiber

VATICAN CITY★**Rome**
(in Rome)

TYRRHENIAN
SEA

M O U N T A I N S

Naples

Sardinia

Palermo

S T R A I T   O F   S I C I L Y

Sicily

M A L T A ★**Valletta**

0   50   100 miles

0 50 100 150 km

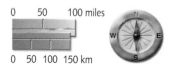

Northern Central Europe

The north of Poland borders the Baltic Sea. It occupies a wide plain, which is cold in winter and warm in summer. This is a land of lakes, forests, rivers, and farmland. Southern Poland's hills rise to the Sudeten and Tatra mountains. The Czech Republic is a land of farms and forests, known for its crystal glass, steel, and breweries. Slovakia's farmland is bordered by the Danube River.

DISCOVER MORE
The highland people of southern Poland are famous for their whirling folk dances. They dance to fast fiddle music at weddings and other family celebrations.

◀ *The twelve signs of the zodiac are shown on this 15th-century astronomical clock in Prague.*

SEARCH AND FIND

Poland		Czech Republic	
★Warsaw	D6	★Prague	F2
Gdańsk	C5	Brno	F3
Katowice	F5	Ostrava	F4
Kraków	F5	**Slovakia**	
Łódź	D5	★Bratislava	G4
Poznań	D4	Košice	G6

COUNTRY FACTS

	Area sq mi (sq km)	Population	Language	Religion	Currency
Poland	120,727 (312,683)	38,199,000	Polish	Catholic	Zloty
Czech Republic	30,387 (78,702)	10,203,000	Czech	Catholic	Koruna
Slovakia	18,859 (48,845)	5,379,000	Slovak	Catholic	Koruna

POLAND • CZECH REPUBLIC • SLOVAKIA

BALTIC SEA

Gdańsk

Vistula

Kaliningrad
(RUSSIAN FEDERATION)

LITHUANIA

BELARUS

GERMANY

Oder

Poznań

P O L A N D

★**Warsaw**

•Łódź

Vistula

SUDETEN MTS.

Oder

Prague ★

Elbe

•Katowice

Vistula

C Z E C H   R E P U B L I C

Ostrava•

Kraków•

•Brno

*TATRA
MOUNTAINS*

UKRAINE

BOHEMIAN FOREST

AUSTRIA

S L O V A K I A

Košice
•

★**Bratislava**

Danube H U N G A R Y

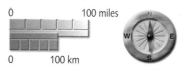

0   100 miles

0   100 km

The Lower Danube

Hungary
Romania
Bulgaria

Hungary's capital, Budapest, is built beside the Danube River, between the highlands, forests, and lakes of the west and the fertile plains of the east. Romania is crossed by the forested mountain ranges of the Transylvanian Alps and the Carpathians. These mountain ranges drop to plains in the south and east, where the Danube River enters the Black Sea. Lowland Bulgaria is also divided by two ranges: the Balkan and Rhodope mountains.

DISCOVER MORE

Europe's largest delta, on the Black Sea coast of Romania, is formed by the Danube River. Its wetlands are home to a variety of birds, from fish-eating eagles to pelicans.

◀ *The Danube River stretches through Hungary's capital city, Budapest.*

SEARCH AND FIND

Romania		Burgas	.........F6
★Bucharest	.......E6	Plovdiv	.........G5
Cluj-Napoca	......E5	Varna	..........F7
Constanța	........E7	**Hungary**	
Iași	.............C6	★Budapest	......C2
Timișoara	........D3	Debrecen	.......C4
Bulgaria		Miskolc	.........C3
★Sofia	.........F4	Szeged	.........D3

COUNTRY FACTS

	Area sq mi (sq km)	Population	Language	Religion	Currency
Romania	91,699 (237,423)	21,698,000	Romanian	Romanian Orthodox	Leu
Bulgaria	42,822 (110,909)	7,974,000	Bulgarian	Non-religious	Lev
Hungary	35,919 (93,030)	10,197,000	Hungarian	Catholic	Forint

ROMANIA • BULGARIA • HUNGARY

AUSTRIA

SLOVAKIA

UKRAINE

SLOVENIA

Miskolc

Budapest ★

Debrecen

H U N G A R Y

Tisza

Cluj-Napoca

CARPATHIAN MOUNTAINS

MOLDOVA

Iaşi

Danube

Szeged

CROATIA

Timişoara

SERBIA AND MONTENEGRO

R O M A N I A

TRANSYLVANIAN ALPS

★**Bucharest**

Constanţa

Danube

Danube

B U L G A R I A • Varna

BALKAN MOUNTAINS

BLACK SEA

★
Sofia

Plovdiv

Maritsa

• Burgas

MACEDONIA

RHODOPE MOUNTAINS

TURKEY

G R E E C E

0   100   200 miles

0   100   200   300 km

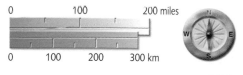

Slovenia
Croatia
Bosnia-Herzegovina

Southern Central Europe

This region of limestone crags and forested mountains borders the Adriatic, an arm of the Mediterranean Sea. Winters in the mountains are cold and snowy, but summers along the coast and its islands are hot and sunny, attracting tourists. The region is rich in minerals and timber, and produces sunflowers, wine, and fruit.

DISCOVER MORE

The limestone rocks of the Postojna cave, in Slovenia, have been eroded by the Pivka River into awesome chambers and pillars, with spectacular stalactites and stalagmites.

◀ *Dubrovnik, Croatia, is on the Dalmation Coast. It is sometimes called "the pearl of the Adriatic."*

SEARCH AND FIND

Croatia	Banja Luka E5
★Zagreb D4	Mostar G5
Dubrovnik H5	Tuzla E6
Rijeka D2	**Slovenia**
Split G4	★Ljubljana C2
Bosnia-Herzegovina	Celje C3
★Sarajevo F6	Maribor C3

COUNTRY FACTS

	Area sq mi (sq km)	Population	Language	Religion	Currency
Croatia	21,829 (56,537)	4,437,000	Croatian	Catholic	Kuna
Bosnia-Herzegovina	19,781 (51,233)	3,989,000	Serb/Croat	SI/SO/Catholic*	Marka
Slovenia	7,821 (20,256)	1,948,000	Slovenian	Catholic	Tolar

*Sunni Islam/Serbian Orthodox/Catholic

CROATIA • BOSNIA-HERZEGOVINA • SLOVENIA

ITALY

AUSTRIA

HUNGARY

▲ *Triglav*
9,393 ft
(2,863 m)

Maribor

Celje

Sava

Ljubljana

SLOVENIA

★**Zagreb**

CROATIA

• Rijeka

Sava

• Banja Luka

• Tuzla

SERBIA AND MONTENEGRO

**BOSNIA–
HERZEGOVINA**

★ **Sarajevo**

ADRIATIC SEA

Dalmation Coast

• Split

• Mostar

Dubrovnik •

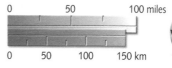

0   50   100 miles

0   50   100   150 km

Serbia and
Montenegro

Macedonia

Albania

Central Balkans

The Balkan peninsula lies between the Adriatic and Aegean seas. It has snowy winters and hot, dry summers. Macedonia is mountainous and lies in an earthquake danger zone. Albania is one of Europe's poorest countries. Serbia and Montenegro are presently united in a federation. Serbia's Kosovo region is under international control after years of strife. The region has mineral resources, and its orchards produce fruit such as plums and cherries.

DISCOVER MORE

Within the Balkans there are two Macedonias. One is the independent nation that used to be a part of Yugoslavia. The other is the northernmost part of Greece.

▼ *Olive groves provide a living for many Serbian farmers who work on the land harvesting the olives.*

SEARCH AND FIND

Serbia and Montenegro
★Belgrade C4
Nis E5
Novi Sad C3
Podgorica F3
Priština E4

Albania
★Tiranë G3
Durrës G3
Elbasan G3
Macedonia
★Skopje F5
Kumanovo F5

COUNTRY FACTS

	Area sq mi (sq km)	Population	Language	Religion	Currency
Serbia and Montenegro	39,517 (102,349)	11,206,847	Serb	Serbian Orthodox	ND/Euro*
Albania	11,100 (28,749)	3,364,571	Albanian	Muslim	Lek
Macedonia	9,781 (25,333)	2,022,604	Macedonian	Mac Orthodox**	Denar

*New Dinar/Euro **Macedonian Orthodox

SERBIA AND MONTENEGRO • ALBANIA • MACEDONIA

HUNGARY

CROATIA

ROMANIA

Vojvodina

Novi Sad

Danube

Belgrade

Serbia

BOSNIA HERZEGOVINA

SERBIA AND
MONTENEGRO

Nis

BULGARIA

CROATIA

Montenegro

Pristina

Podgorica

Kosovo

ADRIATIC SEA

Lake Scutari

Kumanovo

Skopje

Mount Korab
9,025 ft
(2,751 m)

MACEDONIA

Durrës

★Tiranë

Elbasan

GREECE

ALBANIA

0   50   100 miles

0   50   100   150 km

N
W   E
S

Greece

Greece

Greece occupies the southern part of the Balkan peninsula. Its ragged coastline breaks up into many islands, the largest of which is Crete. Fertile plains are hemmed in by mountains.

Hot summer sun, blue seas, ancient ruins, and small fishing villages attract many visitors each year. Greece exports olives, wine, and yogurt. Tourism and shipping are major industries.

▲ The Parthenon in Athens, Greece, sits on a hill overlooking the city. "Acropolis" means the high point of a Greek city.

DISCOVER MORE

The Corinth Canal, with sheer walls of rock, is the deepest cut ever made by engineers. Opened in 1893, it reaches a depth of 1,505 ft (459 m) and is 4 mi (6.3 km) long.

SEARCH AND FIND

Greece	Larissa D3
★Athens E4	Olympia F2
Ioánnina D2	Pátrai E2
Iráklion H5	Sparti F3
Kaválla C4	Thessaloníki C3
Khaniá H4	Vólos D3

COUNTRY FACTS

	Area sq mi (sq km)	Population	Language	Religion	Currency
Greece	50,942 (131,940)	10,940,000	Greek	Greek Orthodox	Euro

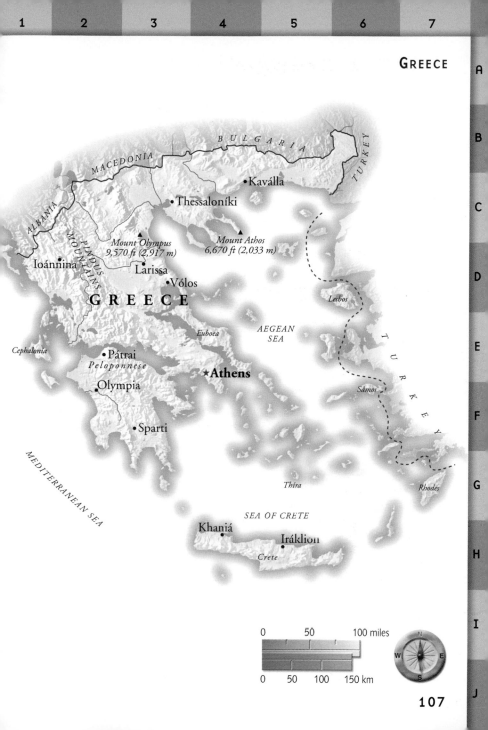

GREECE

1 2 3 4 5 6 7

A B C D E F G H I J

BULGARIA

MACEDONIA

ALBANIA

•Kaválla

•Thessaloníki

TURKEY

Mount Olympus
9,570 ft (2,917 m)

Mount Athos
6,670 ft (2,033 m)

Ioánnina

PINDUS MOUNTAINS

Larissa

•Vólos

GREECE

Lesbos

Euboea

AEGEAN
SEA

TURKEY

Cephalonia

•Pátrai
Peloponnese

★Athens

•Olympia

Sámos

•Sparti

MEDITERRANEAN SEA

Thíra

Rhodes

SEA OF CRETE

Khaniá•

Iráklion
•

Crete

0   50   100 miles

0   50   100   150 km

N
W   E
S

Baltic States

Estonia
Latvia
Lithuania

The states of Lithuania, Latvia, and Estonia all border the Baltic Sea, with its two great inlets: the Gulfs of Riga and Finland. Southern or eastern frontiers are shared with Poland, Belarus, and the Russian Federation. Inland from coastal islands and dunes, most of the countryside is flat, with forests, lakes, peat bogs, and moorland. Farmers raise cattle and pigs. Baltic towns are full of beautiful buildings and architecture.

DISCOVER MORE

The seaport of Kaliningrad, on the southern border of Lithuania, is a part of Russia. It was an historic German city that came under Russian control in 1945.

▲ The Estonian capital, Tallinn, has many buildings dating from the Middle Ages.

SEARCH AND FIND

Lithuania		Estonia	
★Vilnius	G5	★Tallinn	B4
Kaunas	G4	Narva	B6
Klaipėda	G3	Pärnu	C4
Latvia		Tartu	C6
★Riga	E4	**Kaliningrad**	
Daugavpils	F6	**(Russian Federation)**	
Liepāja	F2	Kaliningrad	H3

COUNTRY FACTS

	Area sq mi (sq km)	Population	Language	Religion	Currency
Lithuania	25,174 (65,201)	3,463,000	Lithuanian	Catholic	Litas
Latvia	24,749 (64,100)	2,346,000	Latvian/Russian	Lutheran/Non-religious	Lat
Estonia	17,462 (45,227)	1,370,000	Estonian	Lutheran/NR/EO*	Kroon

*Lutheran/Non-religious/Estonian Orthodox

LITHUANIA • LATVIA • ESTONIA

Gulf of Finland

Narva

★**Tallinn**

Lake Peipus

ESTONIA

• Tartu

RUSSIAN FEDERATION

• Pärnu

Gulf of Riga

BALTIC SEA

LATVIA

★**Riga**

Daugava

Liepāja •

Daugavpils

• Klaipėda   **LITHUANIA**

BELARUS

Nemunas • Kaunas

Vilnius
★

Kaliningrad
(RUSSIAN FEDERATION)
• Kaliningrad

POLAND

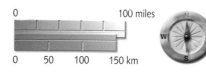

0   100 miles

0   50   100   150 km

Black Sea to the Steppes

Belarus and Ukraine are part of the large plain that stretches eastward into the Russian Federation. Marshes and forests surround industrial towns. The steppe grasslands of southern Ukraine have fertile, black soil, ideal for growing wheat. Many Eastern Europeans take vacations on the warm Black Sea coast. Moldova is a small country of woods and hills, on the western edge of the steppes.

DISCOVER MORE

Optimisticekaja ("optimists' cave") in Ukraine is the world's second-longest cave system. The cave is being explored, and an amazing 125 mi (201 km) has been mapped so far.

◄ *Wild bison, once near extinction, roam the forests of eastern Europe.*

SEARCH AND FIND

Ukraine		Belarus	
★Kiev	E4	★Minsk	C3
Dnipropetrovs'k	E6	Homyel'	D4
Donetsk	F7	Mahilyow	C3
Kharkiv	E6	**Moldova**	
Lviv	E2	★Chişinău	G3
Odessa	G4	Tiraspol	G4

COUNTRY FACTS

	Area sq mi (sq km)	Population	Language	Religion	Currency
Ukraine	233,089 (603,701)	48,416,000	Ukrainian	NR*/Russian Orthodox	Hryvnya
Belarus	80,154 (207,599)	9,951,000	Belarussian/Russian	NR*/Orthodox	Ruble
Moldova	13,012 (33,701)	4,248,000	Moldovan	NR*/Romanian Orthodox	Leu

*Non-religious

UKRAINE • BELARUS • MOLDOVA

LATVIA

LITHUANIA

RUSSIAN FEDERATION

Minsk ★   Mahilyow •

BELARUS

POLAND

Homyel' •

• Kharkiv

★ Kiev

• Lviv

UKRAINE

Dnipropetrovs'k
•
Donetsk

SLOVAKIA

HUNGARY

MOLDOVA

R O M A N I A

Chişinău
★
Tiraspol   • Odessa

BLACK SEA

0   100   200 miles

0   100   200   300 km

N
W   E
S

Russian Federation

Western Russia

The Russian Federation is the world's biggest country. It lies across two continents: Europe and Asia. Most people live in European Russia, to the west of the Ural Mountains. Moscow, the capital, is the center of business and industry. The region stretches from the frozen Arctic Ocean to the warm shores of the Caspian Sea. Most of the region is a forested plain, drained by famous rivers such as the Volga and Don.

◀ *The Peter and Paul Fortress was completed by Peter the Great in 1703, marking the birth of the city of St. Petersburg.*

DISCOVER MORE

Russia's main Arctic port is called Arkhangel'sk, and it freezes over in winter. From November to May, icebreakers are used to keep the shipping lanes open.

SEARCH AND FIND

Russian Federation	
★Moscow E3	St. Petersburg D3
Kazan F4	Samara F4
Nizhniy Novgorod . .F3	Saratov G3
Perm F5	Ufa F5
Rostov-na-Donu . . .G2	Volgograd G3
	Voronezh F2

COUNTRY FACTS

	Area sq mi (sq km)	Population	Language	Religion	Currency
Russian Federation	6,592,800 (17,075,352)	145,182,000	Russian	Russian Orthodox	Ruble

RUSSIAN FEDERATION

Mount Elbrus
Europe's highest mountain
18,510 ft (5,642 m)

ARCTIC OCEAN

BARENTS
SEA

ESTONIA
LATVIA
FINLAND

St. Petersburg

**RUSSIAN
FEDERATION**

BELARUS

★ **Moscow**

Volga

Perm

Nizhniy
Novgorod

Kazan

URAL MOUNTAINS

UKRAINE

Don

•Voronezh

Ufa •

• Samara

Saratov •

Volga

KAZAKHSTAN

BLACK
SEA

Rostov-
na-Donu

Volgograd

Ural

Mount
Elbrus

CAUCASUS MTS

GEORGIA

AZERBAIJAN

CASPIAN SEA

Volga
Europe's longest river
2,292 mi (3,688 km)

0   100   200   300   400 miles

0   650 km

N
W   E
S

See pages 116–117 for Russia in Asia

Asia

Asia is the largest and most densely populated of all the continents.
It forms a single landmass with Europe (Eurasia) and is only separated from the main body of Africa by the Suez Canal. Northern Asia has a bitterly cold climate in winter, with treeless plains (tundra) lying to the north of spruce and birch forests. Across Central Asia is a band of steppe grassland and desert. South of the Himalayas, the world's highest mountain range, are the dusty plains of India and the tropical lands of Southeast Asia.

DISCOVER MORE

Asia is home to the highest and lowest points on Earth: Mount Everest stands at 29,035 ft (8,850 m) and the Dead Sea sits 1,295 ft (395 m) below sea level.

SEARCH AND FIND

Afghanistan	E3	Malaysia	G5
Armenia	D2	Maldives	G3
Azerbaijan	E2	Mongolia	E4
Bahrain	E2	Nepal	F4
Bangladesh	F4	North Korea	E6
Bhutan	F4	Oman	F2
Brunei	G5	Pakistan	F3
Burma	F4	Philippines	F6
Cambodia	G5	Qatar	F2
China	E4	Russian Federation	D4
Cyprus	E1	Saudi Arabia	E2
East Timor	H6	Singapore	G5
Georgia	D2	South Korea	E6
India	F3	Sri Lanka	G3
Indonesia	G6	Syria	E2
Iran	E2	Taiwan	F6
Iraq	E2	Tajikistan	E3
Israel	E1	Thailand	F5
Japan	E6	Turkey	D2
Jordan	E2	Turkmenistan	E3
Kazakhstan	D3	U.A.E.	F2
Kuwait	E2	Uzbekistan	E3
Kyrgyzstan	E3	Vietnam	F5
Laos	F5	Yemen	F2
Lebanon	E2		

ASIA FACTS

Area sq mi (sq km)	% of Earth's area	Population	Largest country by area sq mi (sq km)	Largest country by population
17,400,000 (45,066,000)	30.1	3,718,846,000	Russian Federation 6,592,800 (17,075,352)	China 1,247,761,000

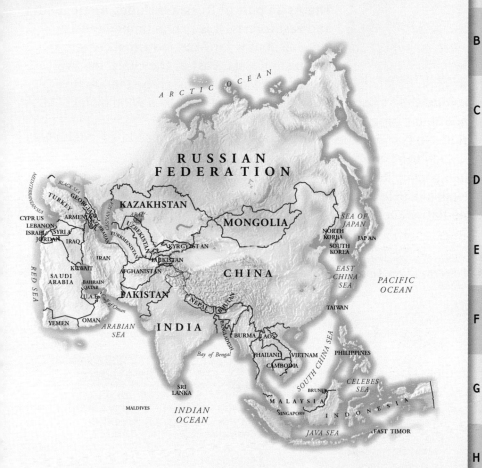

Russian Federation

Eastern Russia

The Asian part of Russia includes Arctic tundra and vast forests. It is rich in timber and minerals, but is far from industrial centers in European Russia. East of the Urals, the West Siberian Lowland is crossed by the Ob River. Beyond the Yenisey River, Central Siberia rises to a wide plateau. High mountains fringe the south. In Eastern Siberia, beyond the Lena River, the volcanic Kamchatka Peninsula extends into the Pacific Ocean.

▶ *The dwindling numbers of Siberian tiger, about 400, survive in the snow-covered mountains of Russia.*

DISCOVER MORE

The Trans-Siberian railroad is the world's longest. It runs 5,772 mi (9,289 km) from Moscow to Vladivostok. This is a week's journey that crosses seven time zones.

SEARCH AND FIND

Russian Federation		
Barnaul	. . . . .G6	Novokuznetsk G6
Chelyabinsk	. . . . . .H6	Novosibirsk G6
Irkutsk	. . . . .E6	Omsk G6
Khabarovsk	. . . . . .C6	Vladivostok C7
Krasnoyarsk	. . . . . .F6	Yakutsk D4
		Yekaterinburg H5

COUNTRY FACTS

	Area sq mi (sq km)	Population	Language	Religion	Currency
Russian Federation	6,592,800 (17,075,352)	145,182,000	Russian	Russian Orthodox	Ruble

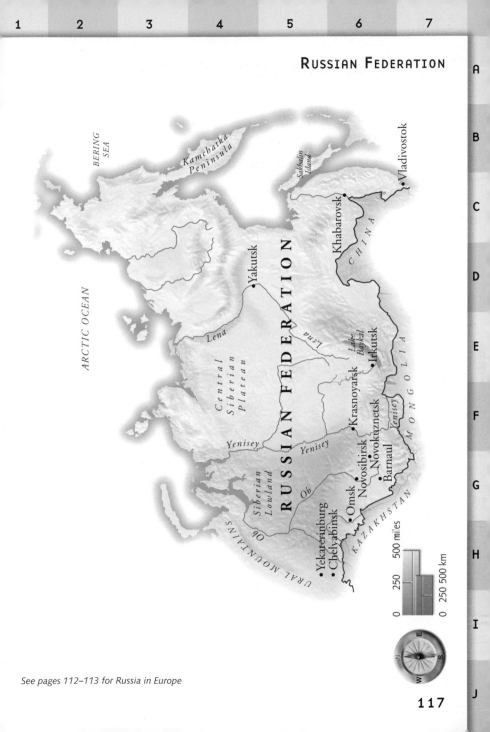

RUSSIAN FEDERATION

BERING SEA

Kamchatka Peninsula

Sakhalin Island

Vladivostok

Khabarovsk

CHINA

ARCTIC OCEAN

Yakutsk

Lena

Lena

Lake Baikal

Irkutsk

MONGOLIA

Central Siberian Plateau

RUSSIAN FEDERATION

Krasnoyarsk

Yenisey

Yenisey

Yenisey

Novokuznetsk

Novosibirsk

Barnaul

KAZAKHSTAN

Siberian Lowland

Ob

Omsk

Ob

Yekaterinburg

Chelyabinsk

URAL MOUNTAINS

500 miles

250

0

0   250 500 km

See pages 112–113 for Russia in Europe

Georgia
Armenia
Azerbaijan

The Caucasus

The three small countries of Azerbaijan, Georgia, and Armenia, occupy the southern slopes of the Caucasus Mountains, which rise between the Black and Caspian seas. This range forms a border between Europe and Asia.

The mountains descend to sheltered valleys, where potatoes and wheat may be cultivated. Grapes, peaches, and figs are grown on the warmer lowlands. Baku, in Azerbaijan, is a center of oil production.

DISCOVER MORE

With an area of 143,243 sq mi (371,000 sq km), the Caspian Sea is the world's largest lake. It is home to the Caspian seal, whose numbers have fallen due to hunting.

◀ *Making carpets for sale in Azerbaijan is an ancient craft, dating back to the 13th century.*

SEARCH AND FIND

Azerbaijan	Kutaisi G4
★Baku B5	Rustavi E4
Gäncä D5	Suchumi H3
Sumqayit B5	**Armenia**
Georgia	★Yerevan F5
★Tbilisi E4	Gyumri F5
Batumi H4	Vanadzor F5

COUNTRY FACTS

	Area sq mi (sq km)	Population	Language	Religion	Currency
Azerbaijan	33,4367 (86,599)	8,141,000	Azeri	Shia Muslim	Manat
Gcorgia	26,911 (69,911)	4,961,000	Georgian	Georgian Orthodox	Lari
Armenia	11,506 (29,801)	3,213,000	Armenian	Armenian Apostolic	Dram

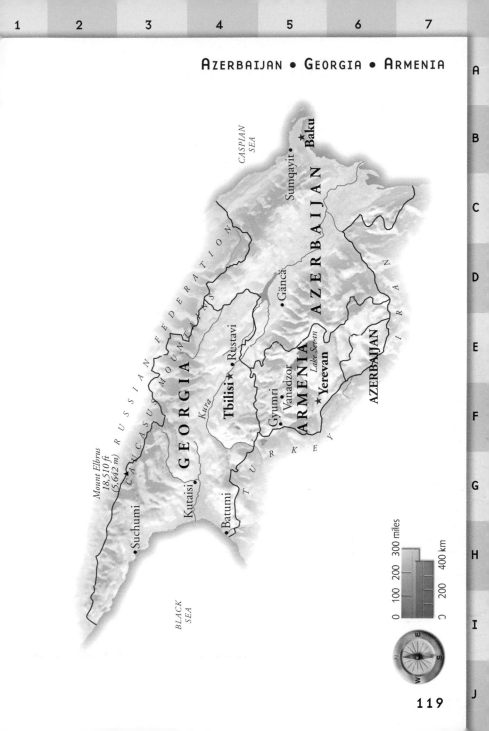

AZERBAIJAN • GEORGIA • ARMENIA

CASPIAN SEA

★ Baku

Sumqayit •

AZERBAIJAN

RUSSIAN FEDERATION

CAUCASUS MOUNTAINS

• Gäncä

GEORGIA

Tbilisi ★ • Rustavi

Mount Elbrus
18,510 ft
(5,642 m)

Kura

ARMENIA

Lake Sevan

Gyumri •
• Vanadzor

★ Yerevan

AZERBAIJAN

IRAN

TURKEY

• Suchumi

Kutaisi •

• Batumi

BLACK SEA

0 100 200 300 miles

0 200 400 km

Kazakhstan

Uzbekistan
Turkmenistan Kyrgyzstan
Tajikistan

Central Asia

Central Asia is a sparsely populated region between the Caspian Sea and the high mountains, which rise to the Afghan and Chinese borders. It is a dry region of steppe grasslands, stony plateaus, and deserts of clay and sand. The peoples of the region include nomadic herders and also farmers who grow cotton or wheat on irrigated lands. Most large towns are in the south of the region, where industries include oil and natural gas.

DISCOVER MORE
Sixteen species of jerboa live in Central Asia. These small, burrowing rodents have very long tails, short front legs, and long hind legs. They can jump up to 8 ft (2.4 m) high.

SEARCH AND FIND

Kazakhstan
★Astana D5
Almaty F6
Qaraghandy E6
Shymkent F4
Turkmenistan
★Ashgabat G2
Turkmenabad G3

Uzbekistan
★Tashkent G4
Namangan G4
Samarkand G3
Kyrgyzstan
★Bishkek F5
Tajikistan
★Dushanbe G4

▲ Farmers harvest cotton plants when the boll dries and the fibers are exposed.

COUNTRY FACTS

	Area sq mi (sq km)	Population	Language	Religion	Currency
Kazakhstan	1,052,100 (2,724,939)	14,952,000	Kazakh/Russian	Sunni Muslim/NR*	Tenge
Turkmenistan	188,455 (488,098)	4,495,000	Turkmen	Muslim	Manat
Uzbekistan	172,741 (447,399)	25,155,000	Uzbek	Sunni Muslim	Som
Kyrgyzstan	76,641 (198,500)	4,699,000	Kyrgyz	Sunni Muslim	Som
Tajikistan	55,251 (143,100)	6,127,000	Tajik	Sunni Muslim	Ruble

*Non-religious

KAZAKHSTAN • TURKMENISTAN • UZBEKISTAN
KYRGYZSTAN • TAJIKISTAN

RUSSIAN FEDERATION

Irtysh

CASPIAN
SEA

★Astana

•Qaraghandy

ARAL
SEA

KAZAKHSTAN

UZBEKISTAN

CHINA

TURKMENISTAN

Shymkent

•Almaty

Ashgabat

Tashkent ★

Bishkek
KYRGYZSTAN

Turkmenabad •

Samarkand

Namangan

TIAN SHAN

IRAN

Amu
Dar'ya

Dushanbe

TAJIKISTAN

AFGHANISTAN

PAMIRS

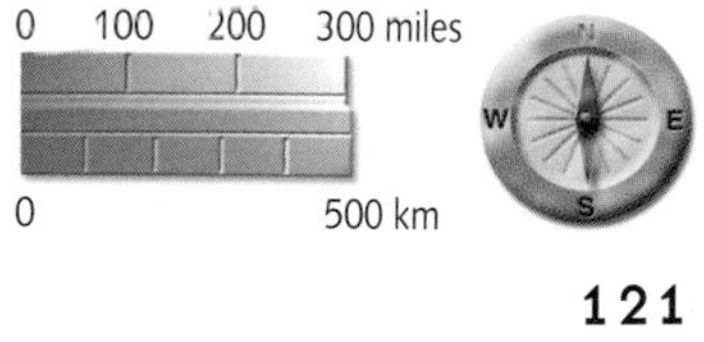

0   100   200   300 miles

0   500 km

N
W   E
S

121

Northwest Asia

Turkey

Cyprus

The Europe–Asia border passes through the Bosporus strait. This is overlooked by the mosques and palaces of Istanbul, which is Turkey's largest city. Turkey's coasts on the Black Sea and the Mediterranean Sea are warm, sunny, and attract many tourists. Inland lies the Anatolian Plateau, hot in summer and very cold in winter. Mountains, lakes, and dusty plains stretch eastward to Iran. The island of Cyprus is divided into two separate territories by its Greek and Turkish populations.

▶ *The Hagia Sophia church, in Istanbul, Turkey, dates from about 532 c.e. and was built in just five years.*

DISCOVER MORE

Millions of birds belonging to about 200 species use Cyprus as a stopping-off point on their annual migrations. Ducks are often attracted by the wetlands of Cyprus's lakes.

SEARCH AND FIND

Turkey		Gaziantep	......E5
★Ankara	........F3	Istanbul	........H3
Adana	..........E4	Izmir	..........H4
Antalya	........G4	Konya	..........F4
Bursa	..........H3	**Cyprus**	
Diyarbakir	.......D4	★Nicosia	........F5

COUNTRY FACTS

	Area sq mi (sq km)	Population	Language	Religion	Currency
Turkey	301,382 (780,579)	67,804,000	Turkish	Sunni Muslim	Lira
Cyprus	3,571 (9,249)	786,000	Greek/Turkish	Greek Orthodox/Sunni Muslim	Pound

TURKEY • CYPRUS

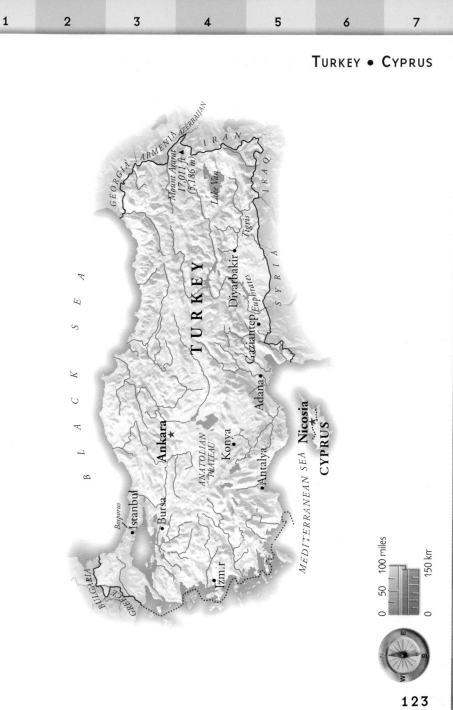

GEORGIA

ARMENIA AZERBAIJAN

IRAN

Mount Ararat
17,011 ft
(5,186 m)

Lake Van

IRAQ

Tigris

SYRIA

Diyarbakir

Gaziantep

Euphrates

TURKEY

BLACK SEA

Adana

Nicosia

CYPRUS

Ankara

ANATOLIAN
PLATEAU

Konya

Antalya

MEDITERRANEAN SEA

Bosporus

Istanbul

Bursa

Izmir

BULGARIA

GREECE

0   50   100 miles

0   150 km

Syria

Lebanon

Western Asia

The eastern Mediterranean coast has warm summers and mild winters. Coastal cities such as Beirut, in Lebanon, are busy centers with large numbers of people living there. To the east of Damascus, the Syrian capital, the land becomes increasingly dry, with vast expanses of deserts. The Euphrates River provides an essential lifeline, allowing wheat and cotton to be grown. Lebanon is crossed by two mountain ranges, between which lies the fertile Bekáa Valley.

DISCOVER MORE

About 4,500 years ago this part of the Mediterranean coast was home to the Phoenicians, traders who invented glassblowing and an alphabetic writing system.

◀ *Trade takes place between the nomadic tribes who inhabit the desert to the east of Damascus.*

SEARCH AND FIND

Syria	Latakia H3
★Damascus H5	**Lebanon**
Aleppo G2	★Beirut I5
Ar Raqqah E3	Baalbek H5
Hamāh G3	Sidon I5
Homs G4	Tripoli H4

COUNTRY FACTS

	Area sq mi (sq km)	Population	Language	Religion	Currency
Syria	71,498 (185,180)	16,729,000	Arabic	Sunni Muslim	Pound
Lebanon	4,015 (10,399)	3,282,000	Arabic	Muslim	Pound

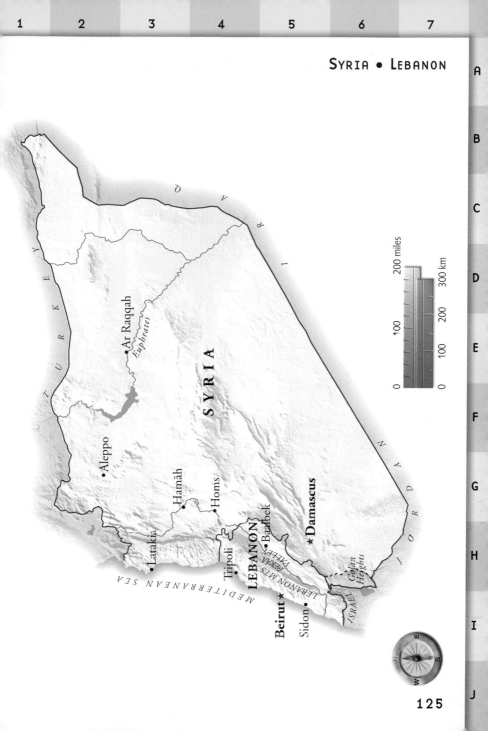

SYRIA • LEBANON

TURKEY

Ar Raqqah

Euphrates

SYRIA

Aleppo

Hamāh

Homs

Baalbek

Damascus

Latakia

Tripoli

LEBANON

BEKAA VALLEY

LEBANON MTS.

Golan Heights

ISRAEL

JORDAN

MEDITERRANEAN SEA

Beirut

Sidon

200 miles

100

0

300 km

200

100

0

N
E
S
W

Israel
Jordan

Jordan and Israel

This region stretches from the warm coast of the Mediterranean Sea, with its groves of olives, oranges, and cypress trees, eastward across the Jordan River. In the east and south are hot deserts. Jerusalem is a holy city to three faiths, Judaism, Christianity, and Islam. Gaza is a self-governing territory, which is home to about one million Palestinian Arabs. The West Bank is also a self-governing territory; its busiest cities are Jericho and Rām Allāh. Peoples of the region, which encounters many political problems, include Jews and Palestinian and Jordanian Arabs.

DISCOVER MORE
The Dead Sea is a lake. Its shores form Earth's deepest exposed depression at 1,300 ft (400 m) below sea level. Its floor plunges to 2,390 ft (728 m) below sea level.

◀ *Thousands of Jewish worshipers visit the Western Wall in Jerusalem.*

SEARCH AND FIND

Jordan		Israel	
★Ammān	D3	★Jerusalem	E2
Al Karak	E3	Haifa	C2
Az-Zarqā	D3	Nazareth	C2
Irbid	C3	Tel Aviv	D2

COUNTRY FACTS

	Area sq mi (sq km)	Population	Language	Religion	Currency
Jordan	34,445 (89,213)	5,230,000	Arabic	Sunni Muslim	Dinar
Israel	7,876 (20,400)	6,631,000	Hebrew	Jewish	New Shekel

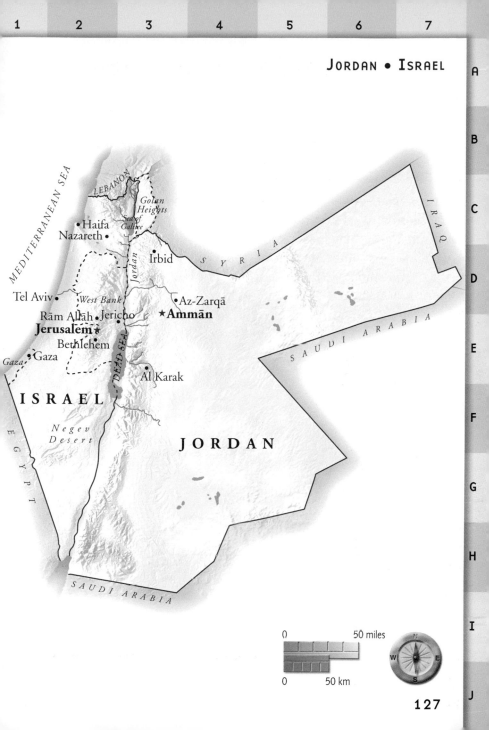

1 2 3 4 5 6 7

A
B
C
D
E
F
G
H
I
J

MEDITERRANEAN SEA

LEBANON

Golan Heights

Sea of Galilee

• Haifa
Nazareth •

• Irbid

S Y R I A

IRAQ

Jordan

Tel Aviv •
West Bank
• Az-Zarqā

Rām Allāh • Jericho
★ Ammān

Jerusalem ★

Bethlehem •
DEAD SEA

Gaza • Gaza

• Al Karak

SAUDI ARABIA

ISRAEL

Negev Desert

JORDAN

EGYPT

SAUDI ARABIA

0   50 miles

0   50 km

N
W   E
S

Northern Arabia

Kuwait
Saudi Arabia

The Arabian peninsula lies between the Red Sea and the Persian Gulf. Nearly all of Saudi Arabia is taken up by hot deserts. The city of Mecca, birthplace of the Prophet Muhammad, attracts millions of Muslim pilgrims from around the world. Saudi Arabia and its much smaller neighbor, Kuwait, have a source of great wealth in their vast reserves of oil and natural gas. Many local people are nomadic herders; others are businesspeople or traders in Riyadh or Kuwait City.

DISCOVER MORE
One part of Saudi Arabia is so barren and remote that it is known simply as the "Rub' al-Khali," the "Empty Quarter." There are no plants, just gravel and shifting dunes.

◀ *The Kuwait Towers, located on the Ras-Agoza cape, were built in 1979. The tallest tower measures 614 ft (187 m) high.*

SEARCH AND FIND

Saudi Arabia		Jeddah	F2
★Riyadh	E4	Mecca	F2
Ad-Dammām	D6	Medina	E2
Al-Hufūf	E5	Taif	F2
Buraydah	D4	**Kuwait**	
Dharan	D6	★Kuwait	C5

COUNTRY FACTS

	Area sq mi (sq km)	Population	Language	Religion	Currency
Saudi Arabia	864,000 (2,240,350)	20,847,000	Arabic	Sunni Muslim	Riyal
Kuwait	6,880 (17,819)	2,228,000	Arabic	Sunni Muslim	Dinar

SAUDI ARABIA • KUWAIT

JORDAN

IRAQ

KUWAIT
★ Kuwait

Persian Gulf

BAHRAIN

HEJAZ

Buraydah •

Ad-Dammām •
Dharan •
Al-Hufūf •

QATAR

N E J D

• Medina

★ Riyadh

UNITED ARAB
EMIRATES

R E D   S E A

SAUDI ARABIA

A S I R

Jeddah
• Mecca
• Taif

Rub' al-Khali

OMAN

YEMEN

0   100   200 miles

0   100 200 300 km

N
W   E
S

Oman
Yemen

Southern Arabia

Both Yemen and Oman are lands of sun-baked mountains and gravelly deserts, crossed by nomadic herders. Coffee and cotton can be grown on highland slopes in the south and west. The southern part of the Arabian peninsula faces the Indian Ocean, and Arabs traded from its ports for hundreds of years. Today, many oil tankers pass through the port of Aden, and the region has rich reserves of oil.

▲ *Minarets (the towers from which Muslims are called to prayer) fill the skyline of Saadah, Yemen.*

DISCOVER MORE

Southern Arabia and the Horn of Africa were the original homes of the coffee plant. It was later introduced to Southeast Asia, India, East Africa, and Central and South America.

SEARCH AND FIND

Yemen		Ta'izz	.........H7
★Sanaa	........H6	**Oman**	
Aden	..........G7	★Muscat	........B2
Al-Ḥudaydah	.....H6	Maṭraḥ	.........B2
Al Mukallā	.......F6	Nizwā	.........B3
Saadah	........H5	Salālah	........D5

COUNTRY FACTS

	Area sq mi (sq km)	Population	Language	Religion	Currency
Yemen	207,286 (536,871)	18,862,000	Arabic	Muslim	Rial
Oman	118,150 (306,009)	2,331,000	Arabic	Ibadhi Muslim	Rial Omani

Strait of Hormuz

★ **Muscat**
Maṭraḥ

• Nizwā

UNITED ARAB
EMIRATES

O M A N

*ARABIAN
SEA*

*INDIAN
OCEAN*

Socotra

S A U D I   A R A B I A

Salālah •

Y E M E N

Al Mukallā •

Saadah •

★ **Sanaa**
Al-Ḥudaydah •

Taʻizz •
Aden •

RED SEA

200 miles

100

0

300 km

100 200

0

Bahrain
Qatar
United Arab Emirates

Gulf States

The United Arab Emirates, Qatar, and Bahrain are three small nations that perch on the eastern coast of the Arabian peninsula. They back up against the scorching deserts of Saudi Arabia and Oman, and look northward across the turquoise waters of the Persian Gulf. All have grown rich from the oil and natural gas industries. Bahrain and Qatar are tiny states, while the United Arab Emirates (U.A.E.) is a federation of seven small emirates (territories ruled by princes).

DISCOVER MORE
Camel racing is a popular sport in the United Arab Emirates. Dromedaries (single-humped camels) are raced over courses at speeds of more than 12 mph (20 km/h).

◀ *Fishermen in Bahrain catch tuna and marlin on dhows (fishing trawlers).*

SEARCH AND FIND

United Arab Emirates	Sharjah D6
★Abu Dhabi E5	Umm al Qaywayn . .D6
Ajmān D6	**Qatar**
Dubayy D6	★Doha D3
Fujayrah D7	**Bahrain**
Ras al Khaymah . . .D6	★Manama C2

COUNTRY FACTS

	Area sq mi (sq km)	Population	Language	Religion	Currency
United Arab Emirates	32,000 (82,880)	4,041,000	Arabic	Sunni Muslim	Dirham
Qatar	4,416 (11,437)	599,000	Arabic	Sunni Muslim	Riyal
Bahrain	268 (694)	651,000	Arabic	Shia Muslim	Dinar

United Arab Emirates • Qatar • Bahrain

Manama
★
BAHRAIN

Strait of Hormuz

OMAN

Ras al Khaymah •

Umm al Qaywayn •

QATAR

Persian Gulf

Sharjah • • Ajmān

★**Doha**

Dubayy •

Fujayrah •

★**Abu Dhabi**

O M A N

SAUDI ARABIA

UNITED ARAB EMIRATES

0   100 miles

0   100 km

Iran and Iraq

The world's first farming began in the green valleys of the Tigris and Euphrates rivers, but much of the rest of Iraq is desert. Its wealth is in oil and natural gas, but a series of wars have devastated the country. Iran also has large oil reserves. It is a land of mountains and deserts, extending from Turkey to Pakistan, from the Caspian Sea to the Persian Gulf.

▲ *Built in 1602, the Si o Se Pol bridge in Eşfahān, Iran, is known as the Bridge of 33 Arches.*

DISCOVER MORE

The country now called Iraq was home to some of the largest and oldest cities in the ancient world. In about 600 B.C.E., Babylon had a population of 350,000.

SEARCH AND FIND

Iran		Iraq	
★Tehrān	E4	★Baghdad	G4
Ahvāz	F5	Arbīl	G3
Eşfahān	E4	Basra	F5
Mashhad	C3	Karbalā'	G5
Shīrāz	E5	Kirkūk	G4
Tabrīz	F3	Mosul	G3

COUNTRY FACTS

	Area sq mi (sq km)	Population	Language	Religion	Currency
Iran	632,457 (1,638,064)	65,540,000	Farsi	Shia Muslim	Rial
Iraq	167,975 (435,055)	27,072,000	Arabic	Shia Muslim	Dinar

IRAN • IRAQ

PAKISTAN

AFGHANISTAN

TURKMENISTAN

Mashhad

IRAN

▲ Mount Damāvand
18,386 ft (5,605 m)

Eşfahān

Shīrāz

CASPIAN
SEA

Tehrān ★

ZAGROS MOUNTAINS

Persian Gulf

AZERBAIJAN

Tabrīz

Ahvāz

Lake
Urmia

KUWAIT

ARMENIA
AZER.

Basra

TURKEY

Arbīl

Kirkūk

Baghdad ★

Karbalā'

SAUDI ARABIA

Mosul

Tigris

Euphrates

IRAQ

SYRIA

JORDAN

200 miles

100

0

0   100 200 300 km

N
E
W
S

Afghanistan
Pakistan

Kabul to the Indus

Afghanistan's deserts and mountains experience seasonal extremes of heat and cold. Most Afghans are farmers. Northern mountains lie across the border with Pakistan, where their snows feed the Indus River and its tributaries. These rivers flow across Pakistan's broad, fertile plains, where wheat, cotton, and rice are grown. Major Pakistani cities include Lahore and Karachi.

People of the Kafir-Kalash tribe in Afghanistan number as few as 3,000. "Kafir-Kalash" literally means "Wearers of the Black Robes."

DISCOVER MORE

Desert valleys or wadis have no rainfall for years and, baked by the sun, become as hard as concrete. When it does rain, water cannot soak into the ground, causing floods.

SEARCH AND FIND

Pakistan		Peshawar	.......D5
★Islamabad	.....D6	Quetta	.........F4
Faisalabad	.......E6	Rawalpindi	......E6
Gujranwala	......E6	**Afghanistan**	
Karachi	.........H4	★Kabul	........D4
Lahore	.........E6	Herāt	.........D2
Multan	..........F5	Qandahār	.......E3

COUNTRY FACTS

	Area sq mi (sq km)	Population	Language	Religion	Currency
Pakistan	307,374 (796,099)	156,483,000	Urdu	Sunni Muslim	Rupee
Afghanistan	251,825 (652,227)	22,720,000	Pashto	Sunni Muslim	Afghani

K2
World's second-highest mountain
28,250 ft (8,611 m)

UZBEKISTAN

TAJIKISTAN

TURKMENISTAN

HINDU KUSH

CHINA

K2

KARAKORAM RANGE

DISPUTED AREA

• Herāt

Kabul ★

Peshawar •

★ **Islamabad**

Rawalpindi •

I
R
A
N

AFGHANISTAN

Qandahār •

Gujranwala •
Lahore •

Faisalabad •

Indus

I
N
D
I
A

Sutlej

• Quetta

Multan •

PAKISTAN

Baluchistan
Plateau

Indus

Karachi •

ARABIAN
SEA

0   100   200 miles

0   100   200   300 km

N
W   E
S

Nepal Bhutan

India

Sri Lanka

Southern Asia

The Himalaya Mountains extend from Pakistan to southwest China and include Mount Everest, the world's highest peak. In two small kingdoms, Nepal and Bhutan, glaciers give way to high, terraced valleys and forests. Melting snows feed the great Ganges River, which flows across the hot, fertile plains of northern India. Central India includes the Deccan Plateau and the Arabian Sea coast. The Western Ghats cover most of this coast. The island of Sri Lanka lies across Palk Strait.

DISCOVER MORE
Elephants decorated with electric lightbulbs glow during the annual Esala Perahera festival in Kandy, Sri Lanka. It is held to honor the Sacred Tooth of the Buddha.

SEARCH AND FIND

India
★New Delhi C3
Ahmadabad D2
Bangalore G3
Calcutta E5
Chennai (Madras). .G3
Hyderabad F3
Jaipur C3
Kanpur D4
Mumbai (Bombay). .E2
Pune E2
Surat E2
Nepal
★Kathmandu C5
Sri Lanka
★Colombo I3
★Kotte I3
Kandy H3
Bhutan
★Thimphu C5

▲ Camels are used to transport goods along the Jamuna riverbank in India.

COUNTRY FACTS

	Area sq mi (sq km)	Population	Language	Religion	Currency
India	1,222,243 (3,165,609)	1,027,000,000	Hindi	Hindu	Rupee
Nepal	56,827 (147,182)	23,078,000	Nepali	Hindu	Rupee
Sri Lanka	25,332 (65,610)	19,410,000	Sinhala	Buddhist	Rupee
Bhutan	18,417 (47,000)	2,124,000	Dzongkha	Lamaistic Buddhist	Ngultrum

INDIA • NEPAL • SRI LANKA • BHUTAN

Mount Everest
World's highest mountain
29,035 ft (8,850 m)

PAKISTAN

CHINA

New Delhi ★

Jaipur •

Kanpur •

Jamuna

Ganges

NEPAL

Kathmandu ★

Mount Everest

HIMALAYA

Thimphu

★ **BHUTAN**

CHINA

• Ahmadabad

Narmada

• Surat

I N D I A

Ganges

BANGLADESH

BURMA

Calcutta •

Mumbai •
(Bombay)

D E C C A N

• Pune

Godavari

ARABIAN
SEA

WESTERN GHATS

• Hyderabad

Bay of
Bengal

Bangalore •

• Chennai
(Madras)

INDIAN
OCEAN

INDIAN OCEAN

Palk Strait

**SRI
LANKA**

Colombo ★ • Kandy

Kotte

ANDAMAN ISLANDS (INDIA)

NICOBAR ISLANDS (INDIA)

0 100 200 300 miles

0 500 km

N
W E
S

Bangladesh
Burma

Bay of Bengal

Bangladesh is a densely populated country.
Its green lowlands produce jute and rice, while
tea is grown in the hills. The Brahmaputra and
Ganges rivers merge to form a delta on the Bay
of Bengal. This is a region that often suffers
from severe flooding during the monsoon season. Burma's chief river
is the Irrawaddy, which also forms a great delta
amidst forests and mangrove swamps. In the
hill country are many forests full of
hardwood timber such as teak.

DISCOVER MORE
Bangladesh has
many historical and
archaeological sites that
date back to the third
century B.C.E. However,
frequent floods have
destroyed much of
the heritage.

◀ *Young
novice monks
in Burma
wear the
traditional
robes of the
Theravada school
of Buddhism.*

SEARCH AND FIND

Burma		Bangladesh	
★Yangon (Rangoon)	F4	★Dhaka	C3
Bassein	F4	Chittagong	D3
Mandalay	D4	Khulna	D2
Moulmein	F5	Rajshahi	C2
Pegu	F5	Rangpur	B2

COUNTRY FACTS

	Area sq mi (sq km)	Population	Language	Religion	Currency
Burma	261,969 (678,500)	45,611,000	Burmese	Buddhist	Kyat
Bangladesh	55,598 (143,999)	129,247,000	Bengali	Sunni Muslim	Taka

Rangpur

Brahmaputra

Ganges

Rajshahi

BANGLADESH

Dhaka

Khulna

Chittagong

INDIA

INDIA

CHINA

B U R M A

Irrawaddy

Mandalay

VIETNAM

Bay of
Bengal

THAILAND

Pegu

Bassein

Moulmein

**Yangon
(Rangoon)**

ANDAMAN
SEA

0   100   200 miles

0   100   200   300 km

N
W   E
S

Southeast Asia

South of China and east of Burma, the Asian continent bulges eastward. In the west of the region, a long and narrow peninsula borders the Gulf of Thailand. The climate is tropical, and rice is grown in flooded paddy fields. Field workers wear cotton clothes and conical straw hats to protect themselves from the Sun and monsoon rains. The Mekong River winds across the whole region, bordering Laos and Thailand and crossing Cambodia and Vietnam.

▶ *In Vietnam, villagers use long, shallow boats to transport their often heavy goods to market for trading.*

SEARCH AND FIND

Thailand	Haiphong B5
★Bangkok E3	Ho Chi Minh City. . .G5
Chiang Mai C2	Hue D5
Nakhon	**Laos**
Ratchasima E3	★Vientiane D4
Udon Thani D4	Savannakhet D4
Vietnam	**Cambodia**
★Hanoi B5	★Phnom Penh F4
Da Nang D6	Battambang F4

DISCOVER MORE
Limestone caves in southwest Thailand are home to the world's smallest mammal, Kitti's hog-nosed bat. It is about 1 in (3 cm) long, with a wingspan of about 4¹/₂ in (14 cm).

COUNTRY FACTS

	Area sq mi (sq km)	Population	Language	Religion	Currency
Thailand	198,455 (513,998)	60,607,000	Thai	Buddhist	Baht
Vietnam	127,243 (329,559)	76,325,000	Vietnamese	Buddhist	Dong
Laos	91,428 (236,799)	5,777,000	Lao	Buddhist	Kip
Cambodia	69,900 (181,041)	12,775,000	Khmer	Theravada Buddhist	Riel

THAILAND • VIETNAM • LAOS • CAMBODIA

C H I N A

Hanoi
•Haiphong

L A O S

Chiang Mai

Gulf of Tonkin

Vientiane

Udon Thani •

Mekong

T H A I L A N D

Savannakhet •Hue
•Da Nang

Nakhon Ratchasima

SOUTH CHINA SEA

Bangkok

C A M B O D I A

• Battambang
Tonle Sap Lake

B U R M A

Phnom Penh **VIETNAM**

•Ho Chi Minh City

Gulf of Thailand

M A L A Y S I A

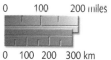

0   100   200 miles

0   100   200   300 km

143

Brunei
Malaysia
Indonesia
Singapore
East Timor

Eastern Seas

A great arc of islands extends eastward from the Indonesian island of Sumatra. The seas they enclose are warm and tropical, the coasts fringed with palms. Crops include rice, rubber, and spices. Brunei's riches come from oil. There are remote forests and farming and fishing villages. Life is very different in large, modern, high-rise cities such as Singapore, Kuala Lumpur, and Jakarta. The region has many volcanoes.

◀ *Singapore contains more than 3,500 skyscrapers.*

DISCOVER MORE
Indonesia is home to about 1,500 bird species and 530 mammal species. However, many of these species are threatened by the destruction of tropical forests.

SEARCH AND FIND

Indonesia
★Jakarta H5
Bandung H5
Medan J3
Palembang H4
Surabaya G5
Malaysia
★Kuala Lumpur . . .I3
★Putrajaya I3

Ipoh I3
Johor Baharu I3
Kelang I3
East Timor
★Dili D5
Brunei
★Bandar Seri
    Begawan F3
Singapore I3

COUNTRY FACTS

	Area sq mi (sq km)	Population	Language	Religion	Currency
Indonesia	735,309 (1,904,450)	206,265,000	Javanese	Sunni Muslim	Rupiah
Malaysia	127,316 (329,748)	23,275,000	Malay	Sunni Muslim	Ringgit
East Timor	5,743 (14,874)	885,000	Tetum	Catholic	Escudo
Brunei	2,228 (5,771)	333,000	Malay	Sunni Muslim	Dollar
Singapore	250 (648)	4,064,000	Chinese	Buddhist	Dollar

INDONESIA • MALAYSIA • EAST TIMOR • BRUNEI • SINGAPORE

PAPUA NEW GUINEA

Papua

Puncak Jaya
16,503 ft
(5,031 m)

CELEBES
SEA

INDONESIA

FLORES SEA

Dili
EAST
TIMOR

Bandar Seri Begawan
BRUNEI

Borneo

JAVA SEA

Surabaya

Kuala Lumpur
MALAYSIA
Johor Baharu
Kelang
Putrajaya
SINGAPORE

Ipoh

Medan

THAILAND

Sumatra

Palembang

Jakarta

Bandung
Java

0 100 200 300 miles

0   200   400 km

N
E
W
S

145

Philippines

Philippines

The Philippines is made up of more than 7,000 islands, many of them volcanic, lying on the western edge of the Pacific Ocean. The two largest are called Luzon and Mindanao. The climate is warm and humid, but cooler in the mountains. Monsoon winds bring heavy rains in summer. There are green forests and ancient rice paddies set into terraced hillsides. Farmers also grow pineapples and sugarcane. The larger cities, such as Manila and Quezon City, are crowded and bustling, and attractive to tourists.

◀ *Water buffalo are traditionally used by rice farmers to assist in plowing fields. Owning large numbers of water buffalo is seen as a symbol of wealth.*

DISCOVER MORE
The Philippines were ruled by Spain for almost 330 years, until 1898. In fact, the islands were named after King Philip II, who was a 16th-century Spanish ruler.

SEARCH AND FIND

Philippines
★Manila D4
Bacolod F5
Cagayan de Oro . . .G5
Cebu F5

Davao G6
General Santos . . .H6
Iloilo F4
Quezon City D4
Zamboanga G4

COUNTRY FACTS

	Area sq mi (sq km)	Population	Language	Religion	Currency
Philippines	115,830 (300,000)	76,499,000	Filipino	Catholic	Peso

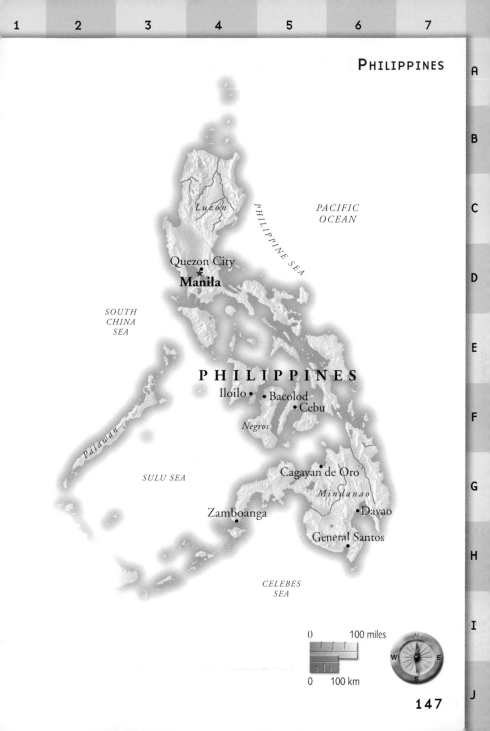

PHILIPPINES

1 **2** **3** **4** **5** **6** **7**

A

B

C
Luzon

PACIFIC
OCEAN

PHILIPPINE SEA

D
Quezon City
★
Manila

SOUTH
CHINA
SEA

E

P H I L I P P I N E S

F
Iloilo • • Bacolod
• Cebu

Negros

Palawan

G
Cagayan de Oro •
Mindanao

SULU SEA

• Davao

Zamboanga •

General Santos •

H

CELEBES
SEA

I

0   100 miles

0   100 km

N
W   E
S

J

147

Mongolia

Mongolia

Mongolia is a land of rolling hills and open steppes that border the empty wilderness of the Gobi Desert, which experiences extremes of cold and heat. Many Mongols are nomads, living in round, felt tents or gers. They are famous as horse riders who herd sheep. They also provide water for the two-humped Bactrian camels, hardy animals that are used as a method of transportation. The camels can withstand the searing temperatures of the Gobi Desert. The only industrial city in Mongolia is Ulaanbaatar.

▶ *The national dress of the Mongols has developed over centuries.*

DISCOVER MORE
The deserts of Mongolia are famous for fossils of dinosaurs, such as *Protoceratops*. In 1922, American scientists discovered dinosaur eggs and nests during an expedition.

SEARCH AND FIND

COUNTRY FACTS

	Area sq mi (sq km)	Population	Language	Religion	Currency
Mongolia	604,247 (1,565,000)	2,373,000	Khalka Mongol	Tibetan Buddhist	Tugrik

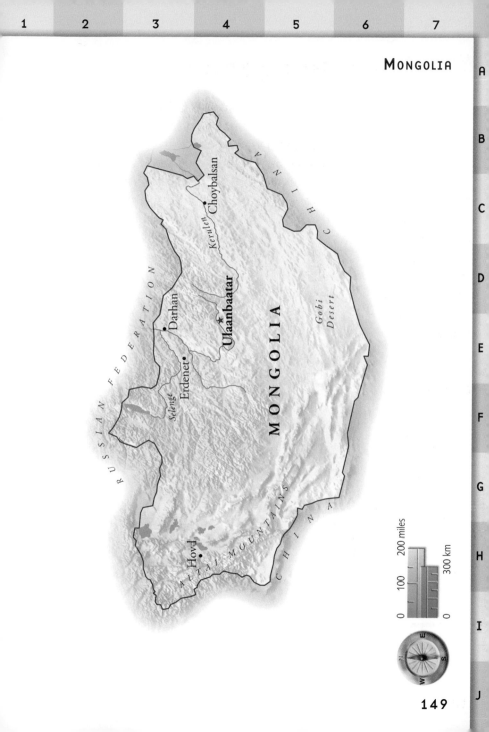

MONGOLIA

CHINA

Choybalsan

Kerulen

RUSSIAN FEDERATION

Ulaanbaatar

Darhan

Erdenet

Selenge

MONGOLIA

Gobi Desert

ALTAI MOUNTAINS

CHINA

Hovd

200 miles
100
0

300 km
0

N E S W

China

Western China

The western region of China is ringed by massive mountain chains. Harsh landscapes include the wilderness of the Taklimakan Desert and the bleak Tibetan plateau. Many people make their living by herding yaks, shaggy-haired oxen that can survive snow and wind. Remote areas are being opened up by loggers, miners, farmers, and engineers. Many non-Chinese ethnic groups, such as Tibetans and Uyghurs, live in the west.

◀ *The often-flooded plains of central western China are broken only by massive rocks emerging from the land.*

DISCOVER MORE
The Chinese name "Taklimakan Desert" literally means "enter and never return." This name has proved to be appropriate because many have gone missing there.

SEARCH AND FIND

China	Ürümqi C4
Hotan D2	Xining D6
Lhasa F4	Yumen D5

COUNTRY FACTS

	Area sq mi (sq km)	Population	Language	Religion	Currency
China	3,696,527 (9,573,998)	1,247,761,000	Mandarin Chinese	Atheist	Renminbi

1 2 3 4 5 6 7

A
B
C
D
E
F
G
H
I
J

KAZAKHSTAN

MONGOLIA

KYRGYZSTAN

TIAN SHAN MOUNTAINS

•Ürümqi

Taklimakan Desert

Yumen

TAJIKISTAN

PAKISTAN

K2
28,250 ft
(8,611 m)

•Hotan

CHINA

Xining

Huang He

INDIA

Plateau of Tibet

Mekong

NEPAL

HIMALAYA

Lhasa

BHUTAN

INDIA

Mount Everest

BURMA

LAOS

Mount Everest
World's highest mountain
29,035 ft (8,850 m)

0   100   200 miles

0   300 km

N
W   E
S

China

Taiwan

Eastern China

In the eastern region of China, mountains descend through bamboo forests to fertile, densely populated plains. Great rivers such as the Huang He and the Chang Jiang flow eastward. The north has cold winters, but the south is warm and humid. Crops include wheat, rice, tea, and fruit. China has many cities and seaports. The island of Taiwan, where most people are Chinese in origin, has a separate government.

DISCOVER MORE

The massive population of China is the world's highest at 1,247.8 million. However, it is now growing at a much slower rate than many other Asian countries.

◀ *Started in the fourth century, the Great Wall of China is 4,163 mi (6,700 km) long.*

SEARCH AND FIND

China	
★Beijing	E5
Changchun	C6
Chengdu	G3
Guangzhou	H5
Harbin	C6
Hong Kong	H5
Nanjing	F6
Shanghai	F6
Shenyang	D6
Tianjin	E5
Wuhan	F5
Xi'an	F4
Taiwan	
★Taipei	G7
Kao-hsiung	H7

COUNTRY FACTS

	Area sq mi (sq km)	Population	Language	Religion	Currency
China	3,696,527 (9,573,998)	1,247,761,000	MC*	Atheist	Renminbi/HK Dollar**
Taiwan	13,969 (36,179)	22,301,000	Min/MC*	Daoism/Buddhist	Taiwan Dollar

*Mandarin Chinese   **Hong Kong Dollar

CHINA • TAIWAN

Chang Jiang
Asia's longest river
3,964 mi (6,380 km)

RUSSIAN FEDERATION

Harbin •

Changchun •

Shenyang •

MONGOLIA

NORTH KOREA

Beijing ★
• Tianjin

YELLOW
SEA

EAST
CHINA
SEA

Huang He

Huang He

Xi'an •

Nanjing •

Shanghai •

C H I N A

Huang He

Wuhan •

Chengdu • Red
Basin

Chang Jiang

Taipei
★

TAIWAN

Kao-hsiung •

BURMA

Guangzhou •
Hong Kong •

SOUTH
CHINA
SEA

LAOS VIETNAM

0   100   200 miles

0   300 km

N
W   E
S

A
B
C
D
E
F
G
H
I
J

Korean Peninsula

The Korean peninsula extends southward from China. It has cold winters, but its warm, wet summers are good for growing rice. The peninsula is home to a single people, the Koreans, but it is divided into two countries. North Korea is mountainous, with plains around P'yŏngyang. Mountains continue across the border into South Korea. Most South Koreans live in the modern cities of the south and west, which produce computers, cars, and electrical goods.

◀ The market economy in South Korea thrives in bustling cities such as Seoul. Little is known about North Korea's economic status.

DISCOVER MORE

Ginseng, known in Korea as insam, is a native plant famous for its healing properties. It has long been used by traditional Korean healers and is popular around the world.

SEARCH AND FIND

North Korea		Inch'ŏn	F4
★P'yŏngyang	E3	Kwangju	H4
Hamhŭng	D5	Pusan	H5
Namp'o	E3	Taegu	G5
South Korea		Taejŏn	G4
★Seoul	F4	Ulsan	G5

COUNTRY FACTS

	Area sq mi (sq km)	Population	Language	Religion	Currency
North Korea	46,540 (120,539)	24,039,000	Korean	Non-religious/Traditional beliefs	Won
South Korea	38,023 (98,480)	48,517,000	Korean	Non-religious/Buddhist	Won

1 2 3 4 5 6 7

A
B
C
D
E
F
G
H
I
J

RUSSIAN
FEDERATION

C
H
I
N
A

•Hamhŭng

**NORTH
KOREA**

*Korea
Bay*

SEA
OF
JAPAN

Namp'o• ★**P'yŏngyang**

Seoul

Inch'ŏn• ★

SOUTH   KOREA

Taejŏn•

*YELLOW
SEA*

•Taegu
•Ulsan

Kwangju• •Pusan

Korea Strait

Cheju Island

0   50   100 miles

0   50   100   150 km

N
W E
S

Japan

Japan

The islands of Japan border the Pacific Ocean. The four largest are Hokkaido, Honshū, Shikoku, and Kyushu. Because these islands are mountainous, most people live on the narrow coastal plains. Crops include rice and tea. Japan has many large, modern cities and is a major world producer of cars and electronic goods. Japan also has many beautiful Buddhist and Shinto temples and old castles.

◀ Japanese temples, such as the Heian Shrine in Kyōto, are usually built with large, tiled roofs, which have long, extending edges curving elegantly upward.

DISCOVER MORE

Like many lands on the edge of the Pacific Ocean, Japan experiences severe earthquakes. Most Japanese buildings are designed to withstand high levels of shock.

SEARCH AND FIND

Japan	
★Tokyo F6	Kyōto F4
Fukuoka G2	Nagoya F4
Hiroshima F3	Osaka F4
Kitakyūshū G2	Sapporo B6
Kōbe F4	Sendai E6
	Yokohama F6

COUNTRY FACTS

	Area sq mi (sq km)	Population	Language	Religion	Currency
Japan	145,882 (377,834)	126,926,000	Japanese	Buddhist/Shinto	Yen

JAPAN

A

B

Hokkaido

Sapporo

C

Mount Fuji
Asia's highest active volcano
12,388 ft (3,776 m)

SEA OF
JAPAN

D

Honshū

•Sendai

E

J A P A N

Tokyo
★
•Yokohama

F

Kyōto
Nagoya
Kōbe • •Osaka   Mount Fuji

Kitakyūshū Hiroshima
•Fukuoka   Shikoku

G

Kyushu

PACIFIC
OCEAN

H

Okinawa
Island

I

0   50   100   150 miles

0   150 km

N
W   E
S

J

Africa

Africa, the second-largest continent, lies between the Atlantic and Indian oceans. To the north, it is bordered by the Mediterranean Sea. The Sahara Desert stretches across most of the north. In the east, chains of mountains and deep lakes lie along the Great Rift Valley. Belts of grassland appear on either side of the steamy rain forests of Central Africa. Tropical rains feed the Nile, the world's longest river, on its journey northward to Egypt.

DISCOVER MORE

The Great Rift Valley—a crack in Earth's crust—runs from Ethiopia to Mozambique. It is more than 4,350 mi (7,000 km) long and, in places, more than 6,000 ft (1,829 m) deep.

SEARCH AND FIND

Algeria	C3	Liberia	E2
Angola	G4	Libya	C4
Benin	E3	Madagascar	G6
Botswana	H4	Malawi	G6
Burkina Faso	D3	Mali	D3
Burundi	F5	Mauritania	D2
Cameroon	E4	Mauritius	H7
Cape Verde	D1	Morocco	C2
Central African		Mozambique	G6
Republic	E4	Namibia	G4
Chad	D4	Niger	D3
Comoros	G6	Nigeria	E3
Congo Brazzaville	F4	Rwanda	F5
Congo, Democratic		São Tomé &	
Republic of	F5	Príncipe	F3
Djibouti	E7	Senegal	D1
Egypt	C5	Seychelles	F7
Equatorial Guinea	E3	Sierra Leone	E1
Eritrea	D6	Somalia	E7
Ethiopia	E6	South Africa	H4
Gabon	F4	Sudan	E5
Gambia	D1	Swaziland	H5
Ghana	E3	Tanzania	F6
Guinea	E2	Togo	E3
Guinea-Bissau	E1	Tunisia	C4
Ivory Coast	E2	Uganda	E5
Kenya	F6	Zambia	G5
Lesotho	H5	Zimbabwe	G5

AFRICA FACTS

Area sq mi (sq km)	% of Earth's area	Population	Largest country by area sq mi (sq km)	Largest country by population
11,700,000 (30,303,000)	20.2	784,445,000	Sudan 967,493 (2,505,806)	Nigeria 111,506,000

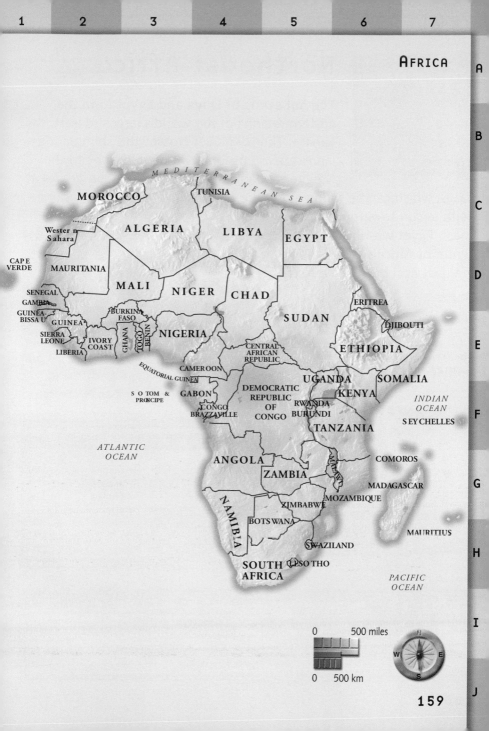

AFRICA

MEDITERRANEAN SEA

MOROCCO

TUNISIA

Western
Sahara

ALGERIA

LIBYA

EGYPT

CAPE
VERDE

MAURITANIA

MALI

NIGER

CHAD

SUDAN

ERITREA

SENEGAL
GAMBIA
GUINEA-
BISSAU

GUINEA

BURKINA
FASO

GHANA

TOGO
BENIN

NIGERIA

CENTRAL
AFRICAN
REPUBLIC

DJIBOUTI

ETHIOPIA

SIERRA
LEONE

IVORY
COAST

LIBERIA

EQUATORIAL GUINEA

CAMEROON

SO TOM &
PRÍNCIPE

GABON

DEMOCRATIC
REPUBLIC
OF
CONGO

UGANDA

SOMALIA

KENYA

INDIAN
OCEAN

CONGO
BRAZZAVILLE

RWANDA
BURUNDI

SEYCHELLES

TANZANIA

ATLANTIC
OCEAN

ANGOLA

ZAMBIA

COMOROS

MADAGASCAR

NAMIBIA

ZIMBABWE

MOZAMBIQUE

MAURITIUS

BOTSWANA

SWAZILAND

SOUTH
AFRICA

LESOTHO

PACIFIC
OCEAN

0　　　500 miles

0　　500 km

N
W　E
S

Libya
Egypt

Northeast Africa

The hot sands of Libya and Egypt form the eastern regions of the world's largest desert, the Sahara. The Nile River crosses this shimmering landscape on its long, winding journey to the Mediterranean Sea. Crops can only be grown at oases, which can be found along the banks of the great river, or in its delta region toward the coast. Egypt was the center of Africa's first great civilization.

▶ *The Egyptian Sphinx is a hand-carved tombstone made out of rock from the Giza Plateau. Pyramids were built as tombs to allow dead pharaohs buried within to reach the Sun.*

DISCOVER MORE

The highest temperature in the world, which measured 136°F (58°C) in the shade, was recorded in 1922 at a weather station in the Libyan city of Al Aziziyah.

SEARCH AND FIND

Libya		Alexandria	D6
★Surt	D3	El Mahalla	
★Tripoli	D2	El Kubra	D6
Al Aziziyah	D2	Giza	E6
Benghazi	D4	Luxor	F7
Egypt		Port Said	D6
★Cairo	D6	Suez	D7

COUNTRY FACTS

	Area sq mi (sq km)	Population	Language	Religion	Currency
Libya	679,358 (1,759,537)	5,605,000	Arabic	Sunni Muslim	Dinar
Egypt	385,299 (997,743)	64,650,000	Arabic	Sunni Muslim	Pound

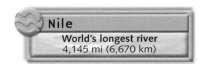

Nile

World's longest river
4,145 mi (6,670 km)

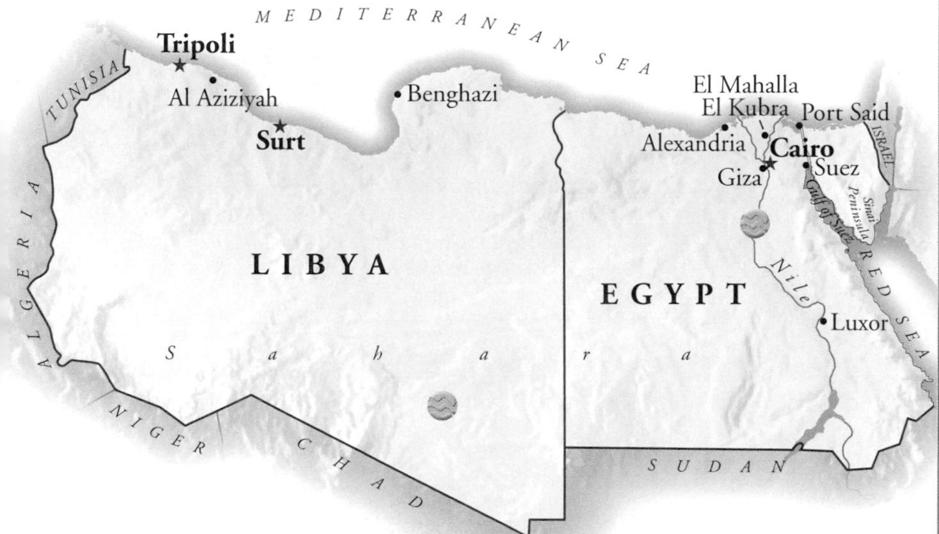
MEDITERRANEAN SEA
Tripoli
Al Aziziyah
Surt
Benghazi
TUNISIA
ALGERIA
LIBYA
Sahara
NIGER
CHAD
EGYPT
El Mahalla
El Kubra
Port Said
Alexandria
Cairo
Giza
Suez
ISRAEL
Sinai Peninsula
Gulf of Suez
Nile
RED SEA
Luxor
SUDAN

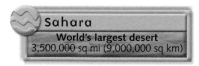

Sahara

World's largest desert
3,500,000 sq mi (9,000,000 sq km)

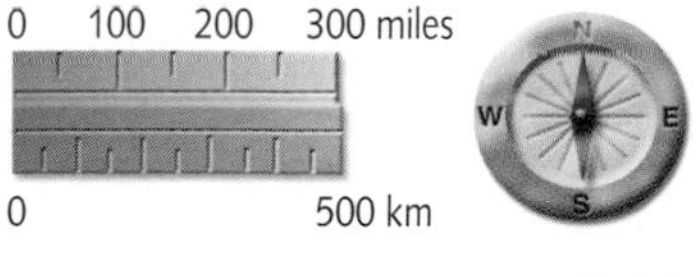
0 100 200 300 miles
0 500 km
N
W
E
S

Morocco
Tunisia
Algeria

Northwest Africa

Morocco, Algeria, and Tunisia are sometimes called the Maghreb. The region is home to Arabs and Berbers. Mediterranean seaports include Tunis, Algiers, and Oran, while Marrakech is one of the chief inland cities. Coastal regions produce oranges and olives, and small farms extend into the foothills of the Atlas Mountains. Beyond the mountains lie the dunes and rocks of the Sahara Desert. Morocco claims the Western Sahara.

DISCOVER MORE
The fennec fox, native to the Sahara Desert, is the world's smallest fox, standing just 8 in (20 cm) high. Its enormous ears add another 6 in (15 cm) to its height.

◀ A fortified wall encircles the ancient town of Essaouira in Morocco.

SEARCH AND FIND

Algeria
★Algiers D2
Annaba C2
Constantine C2
Oran E2
Morocco
★Rabat F3
Agadir G3

Casablanca F3
El Aaiún/Laayoune .H4
Essaouira G3
Fez F3
Marrakech F3
Tunisia
★Tunis B2
Sfax B3

COUNTRY FACTS

	Area sq mi (sq km)	Population	Language	Religion	Currency
Algeria	919,595 (2,381,751)	31,540,000	Arabic	Sunni Muslim	Dinar
Morocco	177,117 (458,733)	30,367,000	Arabic	Sunni Muslim	Dirham
Tunisia	63,170 (163,610)	9,990,000	Arabic	Sunni Muslim	Dinar

ALGERIA • MOROCCO • TUNISIA

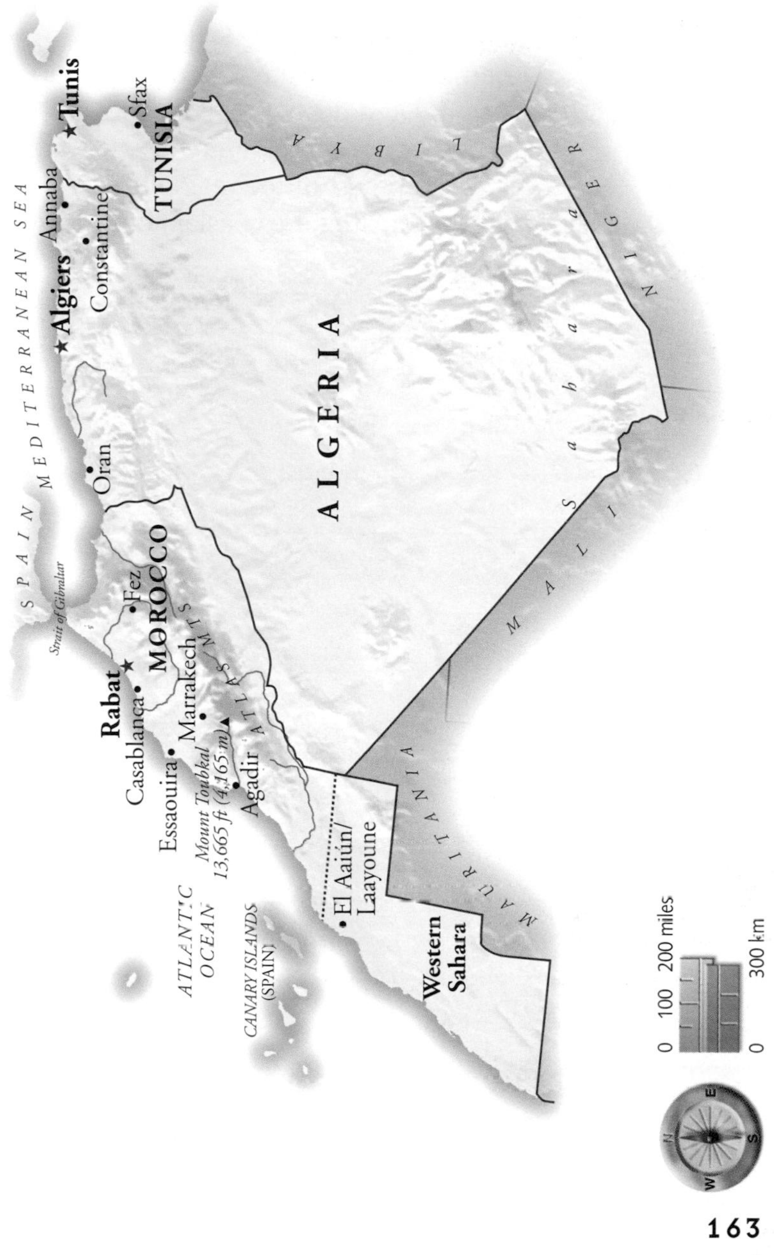

A

B

C

D

E

F

G

H

I

J

MEDITERRANEAN SEA

SPAIN

Strait of Gibraltar

★Tunis

•Sfax

TUNISIA

Annaba

•Constantine

★Algiers

LIBYA

Sahara

NIGER

MALI

Oran

•Fez

MOROCCO

Rabat ★

Casablanca•

•Marrakech

Essaouira•

Mount Toubkal
13,665 ft (4,165 m)▲

ATLAS MTS

Agadir•

ALGERIA

ATLANTIC
OCEAN

CANARY ISLANDS
(SPAIN)

•El Aaiún/
Laayoune

Western
Sahara

MAURITANIA

0 100 200 miles

0 300 km

The Sahel

The region south of the Sahara

Desert is known as the Sahel.
It is so dry and dusty that it is at
constant risk of turning into desert.
The western part of the region has
a more humid climate. The biggest cities are coastal ports
such as Dakar and Abidjan.

1 Mali
2 Mauritania
3 Ivory Coast
4 Guinea
5 Senegal
6 Liberia
7 Sierra Leone
8 Guinea-Bissau
9 Gambia
10 Cape Verde

DISCOVER MORE

The African
giant snail is the
world's biggest land snail.
It can grow to 8 in (20 cm)
long. The largest on record
measured 15 in (39.3 cm)
and weighed 32 lb
(900 g).

SEARCH AND FIND

Mali
★Bamako F4
Mauritania
★Nouakchott E3
Ivory Coast
★Abidjan G5
★Yamoussoukro . .G5
Guinea
★Conakry F3
Senegal
★Dakar E3

Liberia
★Monrovia G4
Sierra Leone
★Freetown F3
Guinea-Bissau
★Bissau F3
Gambia
★Banjul E3
Cape Verde
★Praia E2

COUNTRY FACTS

	Area sq mi (sq km)	Population	Language	Religion	Currency
Mali	428,077 (1,108,719)	11,234,000	Babara	Muslim	CFA Franc*
Mauritania	397,953 (1,030,698)	2,508,000	Arabic	Muslim	Ouguiya
Ivory Coast	124,502 (322,460)	14,786,000	French	Muslim	CFA Franc*
Guinea	94,927 (245,861)	7,430,000	Fulani	Muslim	Franc
Senegal	75,749 (196,190)	9,802,000	Wolof	Muslim	CFA Franc*
Liberia	38,250 (99,068)	3,154,000	Creole	Traditional	Dollar
Sierra Leone	27,699 (71,740)	4,854,000	Creole	Muslim	Leone
Guinea-Bissau	13,946 (36,120)	1,361,000	Portuguese	Indigenous	CFA Franc*
Gambia	4,363 (11,300)	1,365,000	Malinke	Muslim	Dalasi
Cape Verde	1,556 (4,030)	435,000	Creole/Portuguese	Catholic	Escudo

*Communauté Financière Africaine Franc

MALI • MAURITANIA • IVORY COAST • GUINEA • SENEGAL
LIBERIA • SIERRA LEONE • GUINEA-BISSAU • GAMBIA • CAPE VERDE

CAPE VERDE

Western Sahara

A L G E R I A

MAURITANIA

★ Nouakchott

S a h a r a

MALI

★ Praia

Senegal

SENEGAL

Dakar ★

Banjul ★ GAMBIA

Bissau

GUINEA-
BISSAU

GUINEA

Bamako ★

Niger

BURKINA FASO

N I G E R

Conakry ★

Freetown ★

SIERRA
LEONE

Monrovia ★

LIBERIA

IVORY
COAST

Yamoussoukro ★

Abidjan ★

GHANA

*ATLANTIC
OCEAN*

*Gulf of
Guinea*

0 100 200 300 400 500 miles

0 200 400 600 800 km

Nigeria and Its Neighbors

Bordering the Sahara Desert is Nigeria. Farther south, dry grasslands and plateaus are replaced by more fertile soils. The forest zone of the coast produces cocoa, cotton, peanuts, palm oil, and rubber. The Niger River, which gives its name to Niger and Nigeria, fans out through a swampy, forested delta before reaching the Bight of Benin. Nigeria is the wealthiest country in the region, due to rich oil reserves.

◀ *Fishermen trawl with nets in the Lekki Lagoon near Lagos, Nigeria.*

SEARCH AND FIND

Niger
★Niamey E3

Nigeria
★Abuja F4
Ibadan F4
Kaduna F4
Kano E5
Lagos F4
Port Harcourt G4

Burkina Faso
★Ouagadougou . . .E3

Ghana
★Accra F3

Benin
★Cotonou F3
★Porto-Novo F3

Togo
★Lomé F3

DISCOVER MORE
Lake Volta covers an area of 3,280 sq mi (8,500 sq km). Africa's largest dam, it was created by damming the Volta River (south of the lake), and supplies all of Ghana's electricity.

COUNTRY FACTS

	Area sq mi (sq km)	Population	Language	Religion	Currency
Niger	496,900 (1,286,971)	10,790,000	Hausa	Muslim	CFA Franc*
Nigeria	356,668 (923,770)	111,506,000	Hausa	Muslim	Naira
Burkina Faso	105,869 (274,201)	12,603,000	Mossi	Muslim	CFA Franc*
Ghana	92,100 (238,539)	18,845,000	Hausa	Indigenous	Cedi
Benin	43,483 (112,621)	7,042,000	Fon	Indigenous	CFA Franc*
Togo	21,927 (56,791)	5,429,000	Ewe	Indigenous	CFA Franc*

*Communauté Financière Africaine Franc

A

B

C

D

E

F

ATLANTIC
OCEAN

G

H

I

0 100 200 300 400 500 miles

0   200 400 600 800 km

J

Chad
Sudan
Cameroon
Central African Republic

Northern Central Africa

Branches of the Nile River flow through the east of Sudan. In the south, these form a vast swamp called the Sudd. Sudan has the largest area of any African country. Its Libyan and Nubian deserts are part of the great Sahara, which stretches westward across Chad. South of the deserts, cattle can graze on savannah grasslands. In the far south of the Central African Republic (C.A.R.) and in Cameroon are rain forests, where maize, bananas, and yams are cultivated.

DISCOVER MORE

Portuguese sailors explored African rivers in the Middle Ages, and called the crayfish they found there *camarones* ("shrimps"). This is where Cameroon gets its name.

▼ *The natural habitat of some apes, such as the chimpanzee, is under threat in parts of Africa.*

SEARCH AND FIND

Sudan	Moundou F3
★Khartoum E6	**C.A.R.**
Kassala E7	★Bangui G3
Omdurman E6	**Cameroon**
Port Sudan D7	★Yaoundé G2
Chad	Douala G2
★N'Djamena E3	Garoua F2

COUNTRY FACTS

	Area sq mi (sq km)	Population	Language	Religion	Currency
Sudan	967,493 (2,505,807)	31,081,000	Arabic	Sunni Muslim	Pound
Chad	495,752 (1,283,998)	7,651,000	Sara	Sunni Muslim	CFA Franc***
C.A.R.	240,533 (622,980)	3,577,000	Sango/French	Trad/Bap/Cath*	CFA Franc***
Cameroon	183,567 (475,439)	15,746,000	Fang/Murri/French	Cath/Trad**	CFA Franc***

*Traditional beliefs/Baptist/Catholic   **Catholic/Traditional beliefs   ***Communauté Financière Africaine Franc

SUDAN • CHAD • CENTRAL AFRICAN REPUBLIC • CAMEROON

LIBYA

TIBESTI
MOUNTAINS

EGYPT

Libyan
Desert

Nubian
Desert

RED SEA

NIGER

S a h a r a

Nile

Port Sudan

CHAD

Omdurman

Kassala

ERITREA

Khartoum

Blue Nile

N'Djamena

SUDAN

ETHIOPIA

Chari

NIGERIA

Garoua Moundou

Sudd

White Nile

CENTRAL
AFRICAN
REPUBLIC

CAMEROON

Douala

Bangui

Yaoundé

DEMOCRATIC REPUBLIC OF CONGO

UGANDA

KENYA

EQUATORIAL
GUINEA

GABON

CONGO BRAZZAVILLE

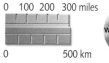

0 100 200 300 miles

0   500 km

Eritrea
Djibouti
Ethiopia
Somalia

The Horn of Africa

Shaped like the horn of a rhinoceros, the coast of northeast Africa juts out into the Indian Ocean. The coasts of Eritrea, Djibouti, and Somalia border a land of hot deserts and scrub, where drought and famine are common and the region poor. In Ethiopia, the deserts rise to highlands surrounding the Great Rift Valley. Here the climate is cooler and rainfall higher. Mountain streams drain into the Blue Nile River. Farming villages grow crops such as teff, and raise cattle.

▶ *The journey home after collecting water from Lake Tana, in Ethiopia, can take up to six hours.*

DISCOVER MORE

At 15,157 ft (4,620 m), Ras Dashen is Ethiopia's highest, and Africa's fourth-highest, peak. Ras Dashen is made of basalt volcanic rock and is one of nine rocky peaks.

SEARCH AND FIND

Ethiopia
★Addis Ababa E3
Dire Dawa E4
Gonder D3
Nazret E3
Somalia
★Mogadishu G5

Hargeisa E5
Kismaayo H4
Eritrea
★Asmara C3
Massawa C3
Djibouti
★Djibouti D5

COUNTRY FACTS

	Area sq mi (sq km)	Population	Language	Religion	Currency
Ethiopia	435,184 (1,127,127)	65,892,000	Amharic/Oromo	EO*/Sunni Muslim	Birr
Somalia	246,201 (637,661)	10,100,000	Somali	Sunni Muslim	Shilling
Eritrea	46,842 (121,321)	4,362,000	Tigrinya	Sunni Muslim	Nakfa
Djibouti	8,494 (21,999)	638,000	French	Muslim	Franc

*Ethiopian Orthodox

ETHIOPIA • SOMALIA • ERITREA • DJIBOUTI

RED SEA

Massawa
★ **Asmara**
ERITREA

ETHIOPIAN
Gonder • ▲ *Ras Dashen*
15,157 ft
Lake Tana *(4,620 m)*
PLATEAU

DJIBOUTI
★**Djibouti** *Gulf of Aden*

Blue Nile

Addis Ababa • Dire Dawa • Hargeisa
Nazret ★ **SOMALIA**

SUDAN

ETHIOPIA

GREAT RIFT VALLEY

K E N Y A

INDIAN
OCEAN

Mogadishu
★

•Kismaayo

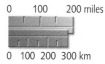

0   100   200 miles

0   100   200   300 km

Uganda
Rwanda
Burundi
Kenya
Tanzania

East Africa

The many landscapes of Kenya, Tanzania, and Uganda include shimmering deserts and rolling savannah grasslands where herds of zebra are hunted by lions. To the west rise the snowcapped tops of Mounts Kenya and Kilimanjaro. There are lakes with hippopotamuses and flamingos. Many tourists visit the game reserves. Crops include coffee, beans, sisal (a tough plant used for its fiber), and bananas.

▲ *The Masai are a famous warrior tribe in Kenya, who live in settlements.*

SEARCH AND FIND

Tanzania
★Dar es Salaam
  (Administrative) . .F6
★Dodoma
  (Legislative) F4
Zanzibar F6
Kenya
★Nairobi D5
Kisumu D4

Mombasa E6
Nakuru D5
Uganda
★Kampala D3
Jinja D4
Burundi
★Bujumbura E2
Rwanda
★Kigali D2

DISCOVER MORE

Covering a total surface area of 26,830 sq mi (69,490 sq km), Lake Victoria is Africa's largest, and the world's second-largest, freshwater lake.

COUNTRY FACTS

	Area sq mi (sq km)	Population	Language	Religion	Currency
Tanzania	364,899 (945,088)	34,569,000	Swahili	Trad*/Sunni Muslim	Shilling
Kenya	224,961 (582,649)	28,687,000	Swahili	Cath/Prot/Trad**	Shilling
Uganda	93,070 (241,051)	24,749,000	Swahili/Ganda	Protestant/Catholic	Shilling
Burundi	10,745 (27,830)	6,490,000	Rundi	Catholic	Franc
Rwanda	10,170 (26,340)	8,163,000	Rwanda	Catholic	Franc

*Traditional beliefs **Catholic/Protestant/Traditional beliefs

Tanzania • Kenya • Uganda • Burundi • Rwanda

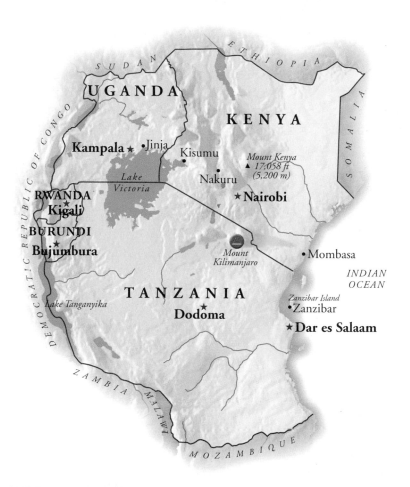

SUDAN

ETHIOPIA

UGANDA

KENYA

SOMALIA

DEMOCRATIC REPUBLIC OF CONGO

Kampala ★ •Jinja

Kisumu •

Mount Kenya
▲ 17,058 ft
(5,200 m)

Lake
Victoria

Nakuru •

RWANDA
★
Kigali

★ Nairobi

BURUNDI
★
Bujumbura

Mount
Kilimanjaro

• Mombasa

INDIAN
OCEAN

Lake Tanganyika

TANZANIA

Zanzibar Island
•Zanzibar

Dodoma ★

★ Dar es Salaam

ZAMBIA

MALAWI

MOZAMBIQUE

Mount Kilimanjaro
Highest mountain in Africa
19,340 ft (5,895 m)

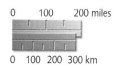

0   100   200 miles

0   100 200 300 km

N
W   E
S

A B C D E F G H I J

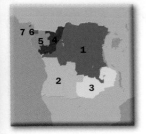

1 Democratic Republic
   of Congo
2 Angola
3 Zambia
4 Congo Brazzaville
5 Gabon
6 Equatorial Guinea
7 São Tomé and Príncipe

Equatorial Africa

The Equator runs through Gabon, Congo Brazzaville, and the Democratic Republic of Congo. The region is partly covered in dense rain forests, with waterways feeding the Congo River on its journey to the Atlantic Ocean. South of the forests are grasslands and plateaus. The southern Democratic Republic of Congo, Angola, and Zambia are all mining countries.

DISCOVER MORE

In the Central African rain forests, some tribal people, such as the Twa, Baka, Efe, and Mbuti, are the world's shortest—some adults grow to just 5 ft 2 in (158 cm) high.

SEARCH AND FIND

Democratic Republic of Congo
★Kinshasa F4
Lubumbashi D5
Mbuji-Mayi E4
Angola
★Luanda G4
Huambo F6
Zambia
★Lusaka D6

Ndola C6
Congo Brazzaville
★Brazzaville F4
Pointe-Noire G4
Gabon
★Libreville H3
Equatorial Guinea
★Malabo H2
São Tomé and Príncipe
★São Tomé H3

COUNTRY FACTS

	Area sq mi (sq km)	Population	Language	Religion	Currency
D.R. of Congo	905,563 (2,345,408)	51,654,000	French/Lingala	Catholic	C Franc*
Angola	481,351 (1,246,699)	12,878,000	Portuguese/Umbundu	Cath/Trad**	Kwanza
Zambia	290,583 (752,610)	9,886,000	English/Bemba	Prot/Trad/Cath***	Kwacha
Congo Brazzaville	132,046 (341,999)	2,943,000	French/Monokutuba	Catholic	CFA Franc†
Gabon	103,347 (267,669)	1,226,000	French/Fang	Christian/IB****	CFA Franc†
Eq. Guinea	10,830 (28,050)	511,000	Fang/Spanish	Catholic	CFA Franc†
S. Tomé & Prín.	371 (961)	138,000	Portuguese	Catholic	Dobra

*Congolese Franc **Catholic/Traditional beliefs ***Protestant/Traditional beliefs/Catholic ****Indigenous beliefs

DEMOCRATIC REPUBLIC OF CONGO • ANGOLA • ZAMBIA
CONGO BRAZZAVILLE • GABON • EQUATORIAL GUINEA
SÃO TOMÉ AND PRÍNCIPE

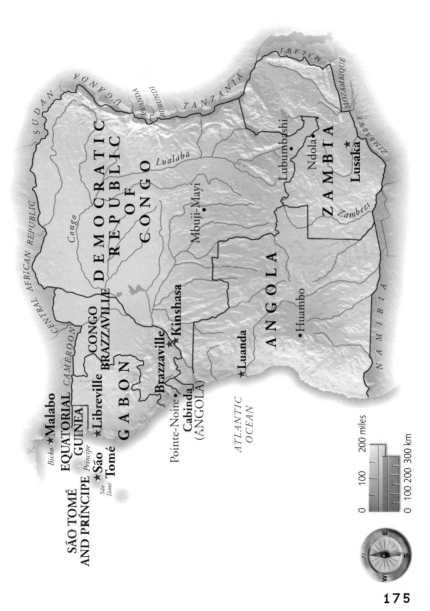

Malawi
Zimbabwe
Namibia   Mozambique
Botswana

Namibia to Mozambique

In Namibia, where the Namib Desert meets the Atlantic Ocean, sea mists roll in over the dunes. The Kalahari Desert occupies western Botswana, but cattle can graze the greener lands in the east. The savannah and farmland of Zimbabwe and Mozambique descend from rocky plateaus to coastal plains. These border the Indian Ocean. Drought and floods are common in this region. The highlands and lakes of Malawi form the southern end of the Great Rift Valley.

▶ The Namib Desert covers one-third of Namibia.

DISCOVER MORE

At the Victoria Falls (Mosi-oa-Tunya), the Zambezi River plummets 355 ft (108 m). This massive waterfall sends a curtain of spray shooting nearly 1,000 ft (300 m) into the air.

SEARCH AND FIND

Namibia		Botswana	
★Windhoek	G4	★Gaborone	E5
Walvis Bay	H5	**Zimbabwe**	
Mozambique		★Harare	D3
★Maputo	D5	Bulawayo	E4
Beira	C4	**Malawi**	
Chimoio	D4	★Lilongwe	C3
Nampula	B3	Blantyre	C3

COUNTRY FACTS

	Area sq mi (sq km)	Population	Language	Religion	Currency
Namibia	318,694 (825,417)	1,827,000	Ovambo/English	Lutheran	Rand
Mozambique	309,494 (801,589)	18,083,000	Portuguese/Makua	Indigenous beliefs	Metical
Botswana	224,607 (581,732)	1,681,000	English/Tswana	Traditional beliefs/AC*	Pula
Zimbabwe	150,803 (390,580)	11,635,000	English/Shona	Ang/Trad beliefs**	Dollar
Malawi	45,745 (118,480)	11,549,000	English/Chichewa	S Islam/Cath/PB***	Kwacha

*African Churches   **Anglican/Traditional beliefs   ***Sunni Islam/Catholic/Presbyterian

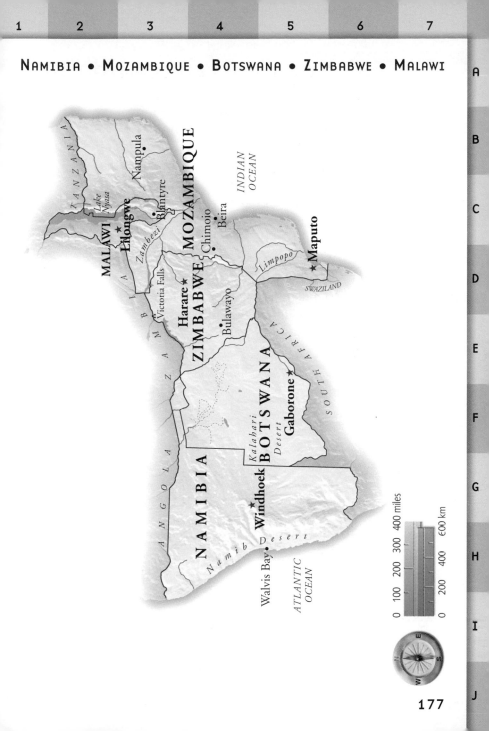

NAMIBIA • MOZAMBIQUE • BOTSWANA • ZIMBABWE • MALAWI

TANZANIA

Nampula

MOZAMBIQUE

INDIAN OCEAN

Lake Nyasa

MALAWI

Lilongwe

Blantyre

Chimoio

Beira

Maputo

Zambezi

Limpopo

SWAZILAND

Harare

ZIMBABWE

Victoria Falls

Bulawayo

SOUTH AFRICA

Z A M B I A

Gaborone

BOTSWANA

Kalahari Desert

NAMIBIA

ANGOLA

Windhoek

Namib Desert

Walvis Bay

ATLANTIC OCEAN

0   100   200   300   400 miles

0   200   400   600 km

Swaziland

South Africa

Lesotho

South Africa and Its Neighbors

South Africa is the southernmost country in Africa. It has large cities, factories, and mines but is also a beautiful country of plateau grasslands (known as veld). It is crossed by the Vaal and Orange rivers, and the Limpopo River forms the border with Botswana. Gold and diamonds are mined, and apples and grapes grow well in the sunny climate of the southwest. The Drakensberg Mountains border two small independent kingdoms, Lesotho and Swaziland.

DISCOVER MORE
Not only does South Africa contain the world's fourth-largest coal reserves, but it is also the world's second-largest exporter of fruit, including mangoes, bananas, and grapes.

SEARCH AND FIND

South Africa
★Cape Town
(Legislative) G2
★Pretoria
(Administrative) .D5
Durban F6
East London G5
Johannesburg D5

Port Elizabeth G4
Soweto D5
Vereeniging D5
Lesotho
★Maseru E5
Swaziland
★Lobamba D6
★Mbabane D6

▲ Giraffes live together in small groups on African grasslands and game reserves.

COUNTRY FACTS

	Area sq mi (sq km)	Population	Language	Religion	Currency
South Africa	471,008 (1,219,911)	44,820,000	Eng/Zulu/Xhosa	Trad/LCC*	Rand
Lesotho	11,718 (30,350)	2,158,000	Sesotho	Cath/Trad**	Loti
Swaziland	6,703 (17,361)	1,008,000	siSwati	LCC/Trad*	Lilangeni

*Traditional beliefs/Local Christian Churches   **Catholic/Traditional beliefs

South Africa • Lesotho • Swaziland

ZIMBABWE

B O T S W A N A

Limpopo

MOZAMBIQUE

Pretoria ★
Johannesburg •
Soweto • •
Vereeniging •

Mbabane
★ ★ **Lobamba**
SWAZILAND

NAMIBIA
Orange

S O U T H   A F R I C A

Vaal

Maseru ★
LESOTHO

Orange

DRAKENSBERG MOUNTAINS

• Durban

ATLANTIC
OCEAN

INDIAN
OCEAN

• East London

★**Cape Town**
Cape of
Good Hope

• Port Elizabeth

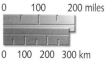

0   100   200 miles

0   100   200   300 km

N
W   E
S

Oceania

Oceania is made up of the landmass of Australia, the large islands of
New Guinea and New Zealand, and chains of small coral islands. These
are scattered across the southern Pacific Ocean. Oceania has the
smallest land area and population of any continent. Much of Oceania
has a warm, tropical climate, but New Zealand lies to the south, where
temperatures are much
cooler. Australia has large
deserts, grassland for
farming, and large modern
cities along its coasts.

▶ *The Great Barrier Reef is a series of
coral reefs that extends for 1,250 mi
(2,010 km). The coral is formed from the
hardened skeletons of dead creatures.*

DISCOVER MORE

Pitcairn is a tiny
island about halfway
between Australia and
South America. Its
inhabitants are descended
from the crew of a 1790
British naval ship,
The Bounty.

SEARCH AND FIND

Australia H5	New Zealand F6
Fiji E5	Palau H3
French Polynesia . .C4	Papua New Guinea .G4
Kiribati E3	Samoa E4
Marshall Islands . . .F2	Solomon Islands . .F4
Federated States of .	Tonga E5
Micronesia G3	Tuvalu E4
Nauru F3	Vanuatu F4

OCEANIA FACTS

Area sq mi (sq km)	% of Earth's area	Population	Largest country by area sq mi (sq km)	Largest country by population
3,300,000 (8,547,000)	5.7%	30,393,000	Australia 2,967,893 (7,686,843)	Australia 19,485,000

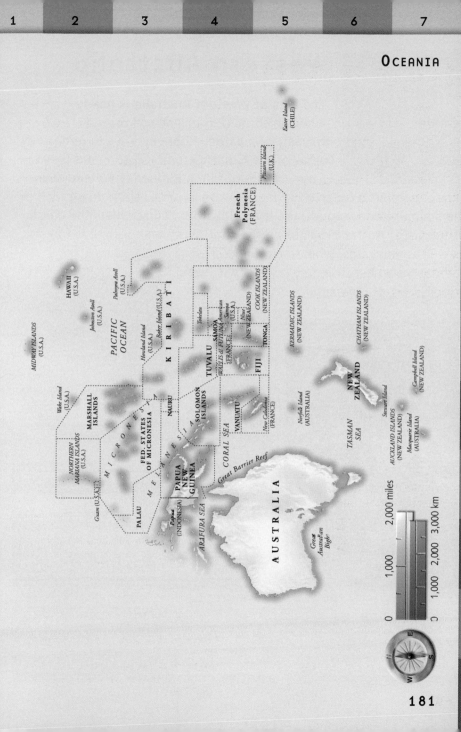

Easter Island
(CHILE)

Pitcairn Island
(U.K.)

French
Polynesia
(FRANCE)

HAWAII
(U.S.A.)

Johnston Atoll
(U.S.A.)

Palmyra Atoll
(U.S.A.)

MIDWAY ISLANDS
(U.S.A.)

PACIFIC
OCEAN

K I R I B A T I

Tokelau

COOK ISLANDS
(NEW ZEALAND)

KERMADEC ISLANDS
(NEW ZEALAND)

CHATHAM ISLANDS
(NEW ZEALAND)

Howland Island
(U.S.A.)

Baker Island (U.S.A.)

SAMOA

American
Samoa
(U.S.A.)

Niue
(NEW ZEALAND)

TUVALU

WALLIS & FUTUNA
(FRANCE)

TONGA

FIJI

Wake Island
(U.S.A.)

MARSHALL
ISLANDS

M I C R O N E S I A

NAURU

SOLOMON
ISLANDS

VANUATU

Campbell Island
(NEW ZEALAND)

NEW
ZEALAND

Stewart Island

AUCKLAND ISLANDS
(NEW ZEALAND)

Macquarie Island
(AUSTRALIA)

Norfolk Island
(AUSTRALIA)

New Caledonia
(FRANCE)

CORAL SEA

TASMAN
SEA

NORTHERN
MARIANA ISLANDS
(U.S.A.)

FED. STATES
OF MICRONESIA

M E L A N E S I A

Guam (U.S.A.)

PAPUA
NEW
GUINEA

PALAU

Papua
(INDONESIA)

ARAFURA SEA

Great Barrier Reef

A U S T R A L I A

Great
Australian
Bight

2,000 miles

1,000

0

3,000 km

1,000   2,000

0

Australia

Western Australia

The area of Western Australia is nearly 1 million sq mi (2.5 million sq km) but is very sparsely populated. Aborigines live in remote areas of the Great Victoria, Gibson, and Great Sandy deserts and the Kimberley Plateau. Miners extract gold, iron ore, nickel, bauxite, and mineral salts across much of the state. In the far south, the level Nullarbor Plain borders the coast of the Great Australian Bight. In the southwest are eucalyptus forests, as well as vineyards, wheat fields, and sheep stations (ranches). The only large city is Perth, with its port of Fremantle.

◀ *Koalas spend almost all their time in eucalyptus trees, either sleeping or eating the leaves and shoots. "Koala" means "no drink."*

DISCOVER MORE

The Elapid family of snakes have venomous fangs at the front of the mouth. The mulga is one of 70 deadly Elapid species found predominantly in Australia.

SEARCH AND FIND

Australia

■ Perth H3	Fremantle H3	
Albany I3	Geraldton G2	
Broome C4	Kalgoorlie-Boulder .G4	
Bunbury H3	Mandurah H3	
	Port Hedland D3	

COUNTRY FACTS

	Area sq mi (sq km)	Population	Language	Religion	Currency
Australia	2,967,893 (7,686,843)	19,485,000	English	Catholic/Anglican	Dollar

1 2 3 4 5 6 7

A B C D E F G H I J

AUSTRALIA

Kimberley Plateau

INDIAN OCEAN

Broome •

Great Sandy Desert

Port Hedland •

AUSTRALIA

Gibson Desert

WESTERN AUSTRALIA

Great Victoria Desert

• Geraldton

Kalgoorlie-Boulder •

Nullarbor Plain

Perth
Fremantle • • Mandurah

Swan

Great Australian Bight

• Bunbury

Albany •

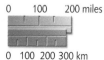

0   100   200 miles

0 100 200 300 km

183

Eastern Australia

Australia

In the eastern half of Australia, hot deserts and rocky wilderness are bordered by scrub and eucalyptus forests. Sheep are raised, and there are successful vineyards. Across the Bass Strait are the forests of Tasmania. Queensland, in the northeast, has pockets of lush rain forest. Tropical fruits and sugarcane are grown there. Most Australians live in busy, modern coastal cities, such as Adelaide, Melbourne, and Sydney.

▲ *Uluru or Ayers Rock is the world's largest rock—standing at a height of 1,100 ft (335 m).*

DISCOVER MORE

The Great Barrier Reef, running parallel to Australia's Pacific coast, is the longest coral reef in the world. Teeming with underwater life, it is over 1,200 mi (2,000 km) in length.

SEARCH AND FIND

Australia		
★Canberra	.....G6	
■ Adelaide	......G4	
■ Darwin	.......B2	
■ Brisbane	......E6	
■ Hobart	........I5	
■ Melbourne	....G5	

■ Sydney	........G6
Cairns	.........C5
Geelong	.......H5
Gold Coast	......E6
Newcastle	.......F6
Townsville	.......D5
Wollongong	......G6

COUNTRY FACTS

	Area sq mi (sq km)	Population	Language	Religion	Currency
Australia	2,967,893 (7,686,843)	19,485,000	English	Catholic/Anglican	Dollar

184

AUSTRALIA

Darwin

Gulf of
Carpentaria

PACIFIC
OCEAN

Great Barrier Reef

Cairns

GREAT DIVIDING RANGE

Townsville

NORTHERN
TERRITORY

QUEENSLAND

AUSTRALIA

Uluru
(Ayers Rock)

SOUTH
AUSTRALIA

Brisbane
Gold Coast

Darling

NEW
SOUTH WALES

GREAT DIVIDING RANGE

Newcastle
Sydney
Wollongong

Canberra

Great Australian Bight

Adelaide

Murray

AUSTRALIAN
CAPITAL
TERRITORY

VICTORIA

Melbourne

Geelong

Bass Strait

TASMAN
SEA

TASMANIA

Hobart

Murray–Darling
Longest river in Oceania
2,330 mi (3,750 km)

0   100   200 miles

0   300 km

New Zealand

New Zealand

A cluster of islands about 1,000 mi (1,600 km) east of Australia in the South Pacific Ocean, form New Zealand. The two largest are North Island and South Island. Auckland and Wellington are centers of industry and population on North Island. South Island's snow-clad Southern Alps can be seen from far out at sea. South Islanders raise sheep and grow fruit. Most New Zealanders are of Maori (Polynesian) or European descent.

▲ New Zealand's lush landscape was perfect for filming The Lord of the Rings trilogy, including The Return of the King (2003).

SEARCH AND FIND

New Zealand

★Wellington	F5	Hastings E6
Auckland	C5	Invercargill H2
Christchurch	G4	Napier E6
Dunedin	H3	Palmerston North . .E5
Hamilton	D5	Rotorua D6
		Tauranga D6

DISCOVER MORE
The kiwi is a flightless bird and the last surviving member of a family called the moas. The tallest of the moas, which died out in about 1850, measured up to 16 in (40 cm) high.

COUNTRY FACTS

	Area sq mi (sq km)	Population	Language	Religion	Currency
New Zealand	107,737 (279,039)	4,009,000	English	NR/Ang/Pres*	Dollar

*Non-religious/Anglican/Presbyterian

NEW ZEALAND

Mount Cook
Highest mountain in Oceania
12,315 ft (3,754 m)

Auckland•

Tauranga
•

Hamilton•

Rotorua
•

N E W
Z E A L A N D

NORTH
ISLAND

•Napier
Hastings

Palmerston
North
★Wellington

TASMAN
SEA

Mount
Cook

SOUTH
ISLAND

SOUTHERN ALPS

•Christchurch

PACIFIC
OCEAN

Waitaki

•Dunedin

Invercargill
•

0   50   100 miles

0   150 km

Antarctica

Antarctica, a continent made of ice and rock at the bottom of the world, is the last great wilderness on Earth. At its center is the South Pole. The land is lashed by blizzards in the winter, and temperatures are bitterly cold. Nobody lives in Antarctica, except for visiting scientists who have set up research stations. They may study geology or coastal wildlife, such as penguins and seals.

▲ Penguins are flightless birds that live on the packed ice of Antarctica. There are 17 different species that are all native to the Southern Hemisphere.

DISCOVER MORE

It is estimated that 90 per cent of the world's supply of fresh water takes the form of Antarctic ice. This is made up of ice caps, glaciers, ice shelves, and icebergs.

★ South Pole

In 1911, Norwegian explorer Roald Amundsen was the first to reach the South Pole. A year later, a British expedition led by Robert Scott also reached the Pole. Amundsen-Scott, a U.S. research station, is now located just west of the Pole.

SEARCH AND FIND

Amundsen-Scott . . .E5
Halley D4
McMurdo G5
Palmer D2
Scott Base G5
Syowa D6
Vostok F5

ANTARCTICA FACTS		
Area sq mi (sq km)	**% of Earth's area**	**Population**
5,400,000 (13,986,000)	9.3	uninhabited

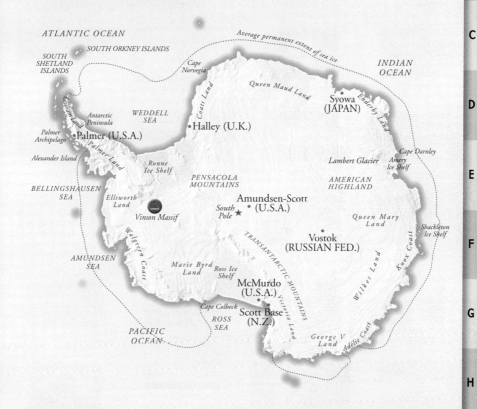

A

B

C

D

E

F

G

H

I

J

Vinson Massif

Antarctica's highest mountain
16,864 ft (5,141 m)

ATLANTIC OCEAN

SOUTH ORKNEY ISLANDS

SOUTH SHETLAND ISLANDS

Cape Norvegia

Average permanent extent of sea ice

INDIAN OCEAN

Queen Maud Land

Graham Land

Antarctic Peninsula

WEDDELL SEA

Coats Land

Syowa (JAPAN)

Enderby Land

Palmer Archipelago

Palmer (U.S.A.)

• Halley (U.K.)

Palmer Land

Alexander Island

Ronne Ice Shelf

PENSACOLA MOUNTAINS

Lambert Glacier

Cape Darnley

Amery Ice Shelf

BELLINGSHAUSEN SEA

Ellsworth Land

Vinson Massif

AMERICAN HIGHLAND

Amundsen-Scott • (U.S.A.)

South Pole ★

Queen Mary Land

Shackleton Ice Shelf

Walgreen Coast

Vostok (RUSSIAN FED.)

AMUNDSEN SEA

Marie Byrd Land

Ross Ice Shelf

TRANSANTARCTIC MOUNTAINS

Wilkes Land

Knox Coast

McMurdo (U.S.A.)

Cape Colbeck

Scott Base (N.Z.)

Victoria Land

PACIFIC OCEAN

ROSS SEA

George V Land

Adélie Coast

• Major scientific base

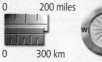

0   200 miles

0   300 km

W   E   N   S

Index of Country Flags

Every country in the world has its own flag. Also shown below are the flags for the states and provinces of the United States and Canada.

Afghanistan

Albania

Algeria

Andorra

Angola

Antigua and Barbuda

Argentina

Armenia

Australia

Austria

Azerbaijan

Bahamas

Bahrain

Bangladesh

Barbados

Belarus

Belgium

Belize

Benin

Bhutan

Bolivia

Bosnia-Herzegovina

Botswana

Brazil

Brunei

Bulgaria

Burkina Faso

Burma

Burundi

 Cambodia

 Cameroon

 Canada

 Cape Verde

 Central African Republic

 Chad

 Chile

 China

 Colombia

 Comoros

 Congo Brazzaville

 Congo, Democratic Republic of

 Costa Rica

 Croatia

 Cuba

 Cyprus

 Czech Republic

 Denmark

 Djibouti

 Dominica

 Dominican Republic

 East Timor

 Ecuador

 Egypt

 El Salvador

 Equatorial Guinea

 Eritrea

 Estonia

 Ethiopia

 Fiji

 Finland

France	Gabon	Gambia	Georgia
Germany	Ghana	Greece	Grenada
Guatemala	Guinea	Guinea-Bissau	Guyana
Haiti	Honduras	Hungary	Iceland
India	Indonesia	Iran	Iraq
Ireland, Republic of	Israel	Italy	Ivory Coast
Jamaica	Japan	Jordan	Kazakhstan
Kenya	Kiribati	Korea, North	Korea, South

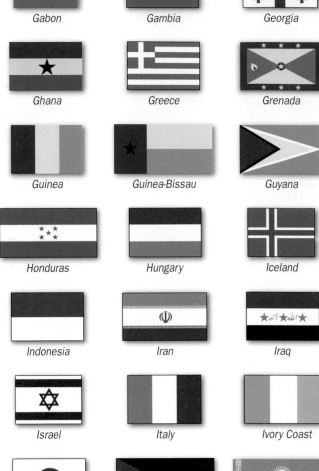

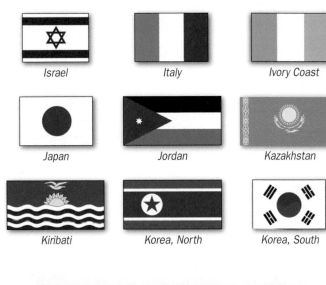
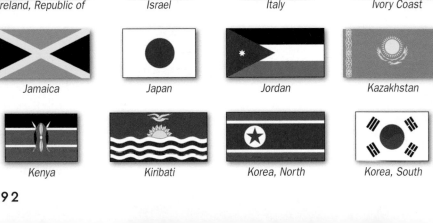

Kuwait

Kyrgyzstan

Laos

Latvia

Lebanon

Lesotho

Liberia

Libya

Liechtenstein

Lithuania

Luxembourg

Macedonia

Madagascar

Malawi

Malaysia

Maldives

Mali

Malta

Marshall Islands

Mauritania

Mauritius

Mexico

Micronesia

Moldova

Monaco

Mongolia

Morocco

Mozambique

Namibia

Nauru

Nepal

Netherlands

193

New Zealand

Nicaragua

Niger

Nigeria

Norway

Oman

Pakistan

Palau

Panama

Papua New Guinea

Paraguay

Peru

Philippines

Poland

Portugal

Qatar

Romania

Russian Federation

Rwanda

St. Kitts-Nevis

St. Lucia

St. Vincent and the Grenadines

Samoa

San Marino

São Tomé and Príncipe

Saudi Arabia

Senegal

Serbia and Montenegro

Seychelles

Sierra Leone

Singapore

Slovakia

Slovenia

Solomon Islands

Somalia

South Africa

Spain

Sri Lanka

Sudan

Suriname

Swaziland

Sweden

Switzerland

Syria

Taiwan

Tajikistan

Tanzania

Thailand

Togo

Tonga

Trinidad and Tobago

Tunisia

Turkey

Turkmenistan

Tuvalu

Uganda

Ukraine

United Arab Emirates

United Kingdom

United States of America

Uruguay

Uzbekistan

Vanuatu

Vatican City

195

Venezuela

Vietnam

Yemen

Zambia

Zimbabwe

U.S.A. State Flags

Alabama

Alaska

Arizona

Arkansas

California

Colorado

Connecticut

Delaware

District of Columbia*

Florida

Georgia

Hawaii

Idaho

Illinois

Indiana

Iowa

Kansas

Kentucky

Louisiana

Maine

Maryland

Massachusetts

Michigan

Minnesota

Mississippi

Missouri

Montana

Nebraska

Nevada

New Hampshire

New Jersey

New Mexico

New York

North Carolina

North Dakota

Ohio

Oklahoma

Oregon

Pennsylvania

Rhode Island

South Carolina

South Dakota

Tennessee

Texas

Utah

Vermont

Virginia

Washington

West Virginia

Wisconsin

Wyoming

*District of Columbia is a federal district, not a state

Canada Province/Territory Flags

Alberta

British Columbia

Manitoba

New Brunswick

Newfoundland and Labrador

Northwest Territories

Nova Scotia

Nunavut

Ontario

Prince Edward Island

Quebec

Saskatchewan

Yukon

197

Glossary

altitude the height of land above sea level.

archipelago a group of islands that are close together.

basin 1. a bowl-shaped area of land that is lower than the surrounding area. 2. an area of land through which a river flows.

bay an inlet in the coastline of an ocean or lake, normally eroded by the waves.

bluff a steep cliff.

border 1. the edge of an area of land or vegetation. 2. the area between two countries. 3. a boundary.

boundary a nonphysical line that separates one country or area of land from another.

butte a steep-sided rock that stands on its own and rises sharply above the land around it.

canal a human-made waterway used for transportation or irrigation.

canyon a deep valley, with steep sides, which often has a river flowing through it.

cape a region of land that projects from the coastline into an ocean.

capital a location officially designated as the chief city of a nation, state, province, or territory, often the center of government.

channel a navigable stretch of water between two areas of land.

cinder cone a cone-shaped volcano that is made from layers of dust and tiny pieces of rock.

climate the pattern of weather conditions normally recorded in any one place or region.

coast land bordering an ocean.

compass rose the points of the compass, as displayed on a map.

continent a landmass or part of a landmass, making up one of the seven major geographical divisions of the world.

coral hard rock that is made from the shells and skeletons of tiny sea creatures.

crag a steep, rough rock formation.

crater 1. a large opening or depression at the top of a volcano. 2. a hollow in the land caused when a meteor crashes to Earth.

crust the thin layer of rock that covers Earth's surface.

current the movement of water over long distances in seas, oceans, and rivers.

delta an area in which a river splits into several separate waterways before entering the sea or lake. It is normally created by deposits of mud or sand. The name comes from the triangular shape of such a region, which looks like the Greek letter delta (Δ).

desert an area of land that has very little or no rain.

divide a ridge or line of crests separating two drainage areas.

earthquake a shaking of the ground that happens when sections of Earth's crust move.

elevation the height above sea or ground level.

Equator an imaginary horizontal line around the middle of the globe, halfway between the North Pole and the South Pole.

estuary a river mouth, where freshwater meets and mixes with the salt water from an ocean or sea.

ethnic group a group of people sharing common descent, language, or culture.

fault line a fracture in Earth's surface along which sections of crust are forced together, or slide past each other, sometimes causing earthquakes.

fjord a long, deep-sea inlet, formed by glaciers in prehistoric times.

floodplain the flat land on either side of a river that is covered by water when the river floods.

forest any large area of dense woodland.

geyser jets of hot water and steam that gush up into the air. They are formed when rainwater seeps into the rocks and is heated by volcanic forces deep underground.

glacier a large body of ice that moves slowly along a valley or down a mountain.

gorge a narrow valley, with steep rocky sides, through which a river runs.

Greenwich mean time the mean solar time of the Greenwich Meridian, used throughout the world as the basis of standard time.

Greenwich Meridian the line of longitude (0°) from which distances to the east or west are measured. It passes through Greenwich, England. Also called the prime meridian.

grid a crisscross network of lines used to locate places on a map.

gulf an area of seawater that reaches into the land. A gulf is usually wide, with a narrow opening into the sea.

harbor a natural or human-made sea inlet that protects boats at their moorings.

hemisphere the globe divided into two halves, either north and south or east and west.

hill land that rises from the ground around it but is not as high as a mountain.

iceberg a large chunk of ice that floats in seas and oceans. Most of the iceberg lies hidden beneath the water's surface.

inlet a narrow stretch of water that cuts into the land from a sea or a river.

island an area of land completely surrounded by water.

isthmus a narrow stretch of land connecting two larger bodies of land.

lagoon a body of salt water that is separated from the sea by a strip of land.

lake a body of water that is surrounded by land.

landlocked surrounded by land on all sides, with no coastline.

latitude the location of a place north or south of the Equator, that is measured in degrees. Measurements are determined using horizontal lines that circle the globe, parallel to the Equator.

lava the hot liquid rock that pours out of a volcano during an eruption.

levee a wall that is built along a riverbank to stop the river from flooding.

longitude the location of a place located east or west of the Greenwich Meridian, measured in degrees. Measurements are determined using imaginary vertical lines, called meridians, which run from the North Pole to the South Pole.

marsh an area of very wet land that is usually low lying.

mesa a rocky hill or mountain with a flat top and steep sides.

mineral a natural substance that is formed deep inside the Earth, for example gold and copper.

monsoon a strong wind that brings heavy rains in the summer months in the Indian Ocean and southern Asia.

moor an area of rough, open, high ground, often boggy.

mountain a very high area of land.

mountain pass a route from one side of a mountain range to the other.

mountain range a chain of high peaks and ridges.

mountain system a chain of mountain ranges, or ranges sharing the same geological origins.

oasis a place in the desert where there is water and some vegetation.

ocean a very large area of salt water on Earth's surface.

paddy a flooded field in which rice plants are grown.

pampas South American grasslands.

peak the highest point of a mountain.

peninsula a strip of land that sticks out into the sea and is almost completely surrounded by water.

pinnacle a column of rock, eroded to a slender point.

plain a large area of flat land.

plateau an area of high ground that is usually very flat.

population the people or the number of individuals living in a given place.

prairie the flat, grass-covered lands of North America.

rain forest forests with dense, evergreen vegetation fed by high rainfall. The term normally refers to tropical forests, but can also mean similar forests in temperate regions.

reef a platform of rocks or coral just below the surface of the sea.

ridge a thin stretch of high ground.

rift valley a long valley created by movement along a fault line in Earth's crust.

river a moderate to large body of water draining off the land and normally flowing between banks toward other rivers or the ocean.

salt flat a large area of flat land that is covered with crystals of salt.

sand dune a hill of sand that is formed by the wind.

savanna a wide grassy plain with a few scattered trees.

scale a distance on a map shown in proportion to the real distance.

scrub an area of land that is thickly covered with low-growing trees and shrubs.

sea a body of salt water, making up an arm or region of an ocean.

solar energy energy that is produced using the Sun's rays.

steppe a wide area of flat grass-covered land in eastern Europe and central Asia.

strait a narrow stretch of water connecting two larger bodies of water.

subtropics the regions bordering the tropics.

swamp an area of wet, muddy land.

territory 1. an area of land that does not have the status of an independent nation. 2. a province or region within a nation.

time zone a large area where every place has the same time. The world is divided into 24 different time zones. The time in each zone is one hour behind or in front of the time in the neighboring zones.

tributary a stream or river that flows into another one during its journey to the ocean.

tropics the warm regions between the Tropic of Cancer and the Tropic of Capricorn near the Equator.

tundra cold, bare land where the soil is frozen for long periods of each year. Only small, low-lying plants can grow on the tundra.

valley a low-lying area, eroded from the land by a river or glacier between two hills or mountains.

veldt the open, grassy plains of southern Africa.

volcano a weak point in Earth's crust, where molten lava bursts through the surface. Lava eruptions may build up to form a mountain.

wetland an area of wet ground.

Dependencies

A dependency is a territorial unit under the jurisdiction of another state, but not formally annexed to it. This list includes only inhabited territories. Some territories are too small to appear on the atlas maps and so their approximate position is given.

Territory (administered by)	Area sq mi (sq km)	Population	Language	Religion	Currency	Page number
American Samoa (U.S.A.)	77 (199)	57,000	Samoan/English	Congregationalist	US Dollar	25, 181
Anguilla (U.K.)	37 (96)	11,600	English	Anglican	East Caribbean Dollar	21, 29 (In the Caribbean)
Aruba (NL)	75 (193)	91,000	Dutch/Papiamento	Catholic	Aruban Florin	65
Bermuda (U.K.)	21 (54)	62,100	English	Anglican/Methodist	Bermuda Dollar	21, 29
British Indian Ocean territory (U.K.)	23 (60)	<10	English	–	US Dollar	23, 115 (S of Sri Lanka)
British Virgin Islands (U.K.)	59 (153)	21,000	English	Methodist	US Dollar	63
Cayman Islands (U.K.)	100 (259)	39,400	English	United Church	Cayman Dollar	63
Christmas Island (AUS)	52 (135)	1,500	English/Chinese	Buddhist/Taoist	AUS Dollar	23
Cocos (Keeling) Islands (AUS)	6 (14)	620	English/Malay	Sunni Islam	AUS Dollar	23
Cook Islands (N.Z.)	92 (237)	18,000	English/Cook Islands Maori	Cook Islands Christian Church	N.Z. Dollar	25, 181
Coral Sea Islands (AUS)	5 (8)	<10	–	–	–	25
Europa Island (F)	11 (28)	<10	–	–	–	23, 159 (E of Comoros)
Faeroe Islands (DK)	540 (1,399)	47,000	Faeroese/Danish	Evangelical Lutheran	Faeroese Krona	21, 81
Falkland Islands (U.K.)	4,698 (12,170)	2,400	English	Anglican	Falkland Pound	21, 67, 79
French Guiana (F)	33,399 (86,504)	181,000	French/Creole	Catholic	Euro	67, 71
French Polynesia (F)	1,544 (4,000)	235,000	French/Tahitian	Evangelical Church of Polynesia	French Pacific Franc	25, 181
Gibraltar (U.K.)	2.5 (6.5)	25,000	English	Catholic	Gibraltar Pound	81, 91
Glorieuses Island (F)	2 (5)	<10	–	–	–	23, 159 (E of Comoros)
Greenland (DK)	840,000 (2,175,600)	56,500	Greenland Inuit/Danish	Evangelical Lutheran	Danish Krona	13, 21, 27, 29
Guadeloupe (F)	687 (1,780)	425,000	French/Creole	Catholic	Euro	65
Guam (U.S.A.)	209 (541)	155,000	English/Chamorro	Catholic	US Dollar	25, 181
Guernsey & Dependencies (U.K.)	30 (79)	62,700	English	Anglican/Catholic	Pound	85 (Channel Islands)
Isle of Man (U.K.)	221 (572)	76,300	English	Anglican	Pound	85
Jan Mayen (N)	146 (377)	<10	–	–	–	27 (Btwn Norway & Greenland)
Jersey (U.K.)	45 (116)	87,200	English	Anglican	Pound	85 (Channel Is)
Johnston Atoll (U.S.A.)	1 (2.8)	500	English	–	–	25, 181
Juan de Nova Island (F)	1.7 (4.4)	<10	–	–	–	23, 159 (E of Comoros)

	Area sq mi (sq km)	Population	Language	Religion	Currency	Page number
Kerguelen Islands (F)	3,000 (7,785)	145	–	–	–	23
Martinique (F)	436 (1,129)	381,000	French/Creole	Catholic	Euro	65
Mayotte (F)	145 (376)	160,000	French/Mahorian	Sunni Islam	Euro	23, 159 (E of Comoros)
Midway Islands (U.S.A.)	2 (5)	40	–	–	–	25, 181
Montserrat (U.K.)	38 (98)	5,000	English	Anglican	East Caribbean Dollar	65
Netherlands Antilles (NL)	309 (800)	176,000	Dutch/ Papiamento/English	Catholic	Netherlands Antilles Guilder or Florin	65
New Caledonia (F)	7,172 (18,576)	208,000	French	Catholic	French Pacific Franc	25, 181
Niue (N.Z.)	100 (259)	1,800	English/Niuean	Cong. Niue Church	N.Z. Dollar	25, 181
Norfolk Island (AUS)	13 (35)	2,000	English/Norfolk Island	Anglican	AUS Dollar	25, 181
Northern Mariana Islands (U.S.A.)	184 (477)	69,000	English/ Chamorro/Filipino	Catholic	US Dollar	25, 181
Palmyra Atoll (U.S.A.)	4.5 (12)	20	–	–	–	181
Pitcairn (U.K.)	18 (47)	47	Pitkern	Seventh-day Adventist	N.Z. Dollar	25, 181
Puerto Rico (U.S.A.)	3,515 (9,104)	3,859,000	Spanish/English	Catholic	US Dollar	63
Réunion (F)	969 (2,510)	699,000	French/Creole	Catholic	Euro	23
St. Helena & Dependencies (U.K.)	159 (411)	7,000	English	Anglican/Baptist	Pound (local issue)	21
St. Pierre & Miquelon (F)	93 (242)	6,300	French	Catholic	Euro	21, 29 (SW of Newfoundland)
South Georgia & South Sandwich Islands (U.K.)	1,580 (4,091)	<10	–	–	–	21
Svalbard (N)	24,273 (62,703)	2,900	Norwegian/ Russian/Ukrainian	Evangelical Lutheran	Krone	27
Tokelau (N.Z.)	5 (13)	1,500	English/ Tokelauan	Congregationalist	N.Z. Dollar	25, 181
Turks & Caicos Islands (U.K.)	166 (430)	20,000	English	Baptist/Anglican	US Dollar	63
Virgin Islands of the U.S.A. (U.S.A.)	136 (352)	109,000	English/Spanish	Baptist/Catholic	US Dollar	63
Wallis & Futuna (F)	106 (274)	15,000	French/Wallisian/ Futunian	Catholic	French Pacific Franc	25, 181

Key

Aus = Australia   DK = Denmark   F = France   N = Norway   NL = Netherlands   N.Z. = New Zealand   U.K. = United Kingdom   U.S.A. = United States of America

Btwn = Between   Cong. = Congregational   < = Fewer than

Disputed Territories

The following are dependencies that are disputed. Various states claim them.

Territory (claimed by)	Area sq mi (sq km)	Population	Language	Religion	Currency	Page number
Gaza and West Bank	2,146 (6,257)	3,040,000	Arabic	Sunni Islam/ Christianity	New Israeli Shekel	126, 127
Golan Heights	444 (1,150)	33,000	Hebrew/Arabic	Sunni Islam/ Jewish	New Israeli Shekel	127
Western Sahara (Morocco/ Polisario guerilla movement)	102,700 (266,000)	256,000	Arabic	Sunni Islam	Moroccan Dirham	163

Index

Numbers in **bold** type refer to main entries. Numbers in *italics* refer to illustrations.

Bahamas 29 G6, **62–63**, *62,* 190

Bahrain 115 E2, **132–133**, *132,* 190

Baja California (peninsula) Mexico 59 H4

Baker Island Pacific Ocean 181 E3

Bakersfield California, U.S.A. 49 G3

Baku Azerbaijan 118, 119 B5

Balearic Islands Spain 91 E7

Balkan Mountains Bulgaria 100, 101 F5

Balkans 80, **104–105**

Balkhash, Lake Kazakhstan 19

Baltic Sea 19, 20, 81, 83, 92, 98, 99, 108, 109

Baltic States 108–109

Baltimore Maryland, U.S.A. 35 F5

Baluchistan Plateau Pakistan 137 G2

Bamako Mali 165 F4

Bandar Seri Begawan Brunei 145 F3

Bandung Indonesia 145 H5

Banff National Park Canada *52*

Bangalore India 139 G3

Bangkok Thailand 143 E3

Bangladesh 115 F4, **140–141**, 190

Bangui Central African Republic 169 G3

Banja Luka Bosnia-Herzegovina 103 E5

Banjul Gambia 165 E3

Banks Island Northwest Territories, Canada 27 D3

Barbados 29 G7, **64–65**, 190

Barbuda 29 G7, **64–65**

Barcelona Spain 91 D6

Barents Sea 19, 27, 113

Barnaul Russian Federation 117 G6

Barquisimeto Venezuela 69 C4

Barranquilla Colombia 69 C3

Barrow Alaska, U.S.A. 27 D3

Barrow, Point Alaska, U.S.A. 27 D4

Basel Switzerland 95 I3

Basra Iraq 135 F5

Bass Strait Australia 184, 185 H5

Bassein Burma 141 F4

Basseterre St. Kitts-Nevis 65 D5

Bathurst, Cape Nunavut, Canada 27 D3

Baton Rouge Louisiana, U.S.A. 37 F3

Battambang Cambodia 143 F4

Batumi Georgia 119 H4

Bavarian Alps Germany 92, 93 H4

Baykal, Lake Russian Federation 19, 117 E6

Beaufort Sea 18, 27 D3, 29 C3

Beijing China 153 E5

Beira Mozambique 177 C4

Beirut Lebanon 124, 125 I5

Bekáa Valley Lebanon 124, 125 H5

Belarus 81 E5, 108, **110–111**, 190

Belém Brazil 73 D5

Belfast U.K. 85 E3

Belgium 81 E3, **86–87**, 190

Belgrade Serbia and Montenegro 105 C4

Belize 29 G5, **60–61**, 190

Belize City Belize 61 G2

Bellingshausen Sea 189 E2

Belmopan Belize 61 G2

Belo Horizonte Brazil 73 G6

Bengal, Bay of India 19, 23 C6, 115 G4, 139 E5, **140–141**

Benghazi Libya 161 D4

Beni (river) Bolivia 77 C2

Benin 159 E3, **166–167**, 190

Benue (river) Cameroon/ Nigeria 167 F5

Bergen Norway 83 F2

Bering Sea 19, 25, 31, 117

Bering Strait Arctic Ocean/ Pacific Ocean 27 C4, 51 B3

Berlin Germany 93 D6

Bermuda (island) Atlantic Ocean 21 E3, 29 F6, 200

Bern Switzerland 95 I4

Bernese Alps Switzerland 95 I5

Bethlehem Israel 127 E2

Bhutan 115 F4, **138–139**, 190

Bighorn Mountains Wyoming, U.S.A. 47 D5

Bight of Benin 166, 167 G3

Bilbao Spain 91 C4

Billings Montana, U.S.A. 47 D5

Bioko (island) Equatorial Guinea 21 F6, 175 H2

Birmingham Alabama, U.S.A. 37 E4

Birmingham U.K. 85 G5

Biscay, Bay of Spain 81 F2, 91 B4

Bishkek Kyrgyzstan 121 F5

Bismarck North Dakota, U.S.A. 43 D3

Bissau Guinea-Bissau 165 F3

Black Forest (mountain range) Germany 93 G3

Black Sea 19, 81, 100, 101, **110–111**, 113, 115, 118, 119, 123

Blanc, Mont (mountain) France 89 E6, 89

Blanco, Cape Oregon, U.S.A. 21 H3

Blantyre Malawi 177 C3

Blue Nile (river) Ethiopia/ Sudan 169 E6, 170, 171 E3

Bogotá Colombia 68, *68,* 69 E3

Boise Idaho, U.S.A. 47 D3

Bolívar, Pico (mountain) Venezuela 69 D4

Bolivia 67 E3, **76–77**, *76,* 190

Bonaire (island) Netherlands Antilles 65 F4

Easter Island Pacific Ocean
25 G6, 181 B5
Eastern Australia 184–185
Eastern Canada 54–55
Eastern China 152–153
Eastern Europe 110–111
Eastern Russia 116–117
Eastern Seas 144–145
Ebro (river) Spain 91 C4 &
D6
Ecuador 67 C2, 74–75, 191
Edinburgh U.K. 85 D4
Edmonton Alberta, Canada
53 G5, 57 G3
Egypt 159 C5, 160–161, 191
Eindhoven Netherlands
87 E5
El Aaiún Western Sahara
163 H4
El Mahalla El Kubra Egypt
161 D6
El Paso Texas, U.S.A. 41 E3
El Salvador 29 H5, 60–61,
191
Elbasan Albania 105 G3
Elbe (river) Czech Republic/
Germany 92, 93 C5 &
E7, 99 F3
Elbrus, Mount Russian
Federation 80, 113 H1,
119 G3
Ellesmere Island Nunavut,
Canada 18, 27 E3
Ellsworth Land Antarctica
189 E2
Encarnación Paraguay 77 H7
Enderby Land Antarctica
189 D6
England U.K. 84–85, 85 G5
English Channel 85 H4, 88,
89
Equatorial Africa 174–175
Equatorial Guinea 159 E3,
174–175, 191
Erdenet Mongolia 149 E3
Erie Pennsylvania, U.S.A.
35 D2
Eric, Lake Canada/U.S.A. 34,
35 D2, 45 E6
Eritrea 159 D6, 170–171, 191

Eşfahān Iran 134, 135 E4
Essaouira Morocco 162, 163
G3
Essen Germany 93 E3
Essequibo (river) Guyana
71 F3
Estonia 81 D5, 108–109, 191
Ethiopia 159 E6, 170,
170–171, 191
Ethiopian Highlands 19
Ethiopian Plateau 171 D3
Euboea (island) Greece
107 E4
Eugene Oregon, U.S.A.
49 D3
Euphrates (river) Asia 19,
123 D5, 124, 125 E3,
134, 135 G5
Europa Island 200
Europe 19, 80–81, 112
Alps 94–95
Balkans 104–105
Caucasus 80, 118–119
Eastern Europe 110–111
France 88–89
Iberian Peninsula 90–91
Northern Central 98–99
Russian Federation 112–113
Southern Central 102–103
European Plain 19
Everest, Mount China/Nepal
12, 114, 138, 139 C5
Everglades, The Florida,
U.S.A. 36, 37 G6

F

Faeroe Islands Atlantic Ocean
21 C5, 81 C2, 200
Fairbanks Alaska, U.S.A.
51 B5
Faisalabad Pakistan 137 E6
Falkland Islands Atlantic
Ocean 18, 21 H3, 67 H4,
79 H4, 200
Farewell, Cape Greenland
21 C4
Fargo North Dakota, U.S.A.
43 D4
Fayetteville Arkansas, U.S.A.
37 D2

Federated States of
Micronesia 25 F2,
181 G3
Fernando de Noronha Island
Brazil 21 F5, 67 D7
Fez Morocco 163 F3
Fiji 24–25, 25 G3, 181 E5,
191
Finisterre, Cape Spain 21 D5
Finland 81 D5, 82–83, 191
Finland, Gulf of 108, 109 B4
flags 190–197
Flint Michigan, U.S.A. 45 E5
Florence Italy 97 D4
Flores Sea 145 E5
Florida (state) U.S.A. 31 C6,
36–37, 196
Florida Keys Florida, U.S.A.
31 C7, 37 G6
Fort Delaware Delaware,
U.S.A. 34
Fort Wayne Indiana, U.S.A.
45 F5
Fortaleza Brazil 73 D7
Foxe Basin Canada 27 F2
France 81 F3, 88, 88–89, 92,
192
Frankfort Kentucky, U.S.A.
39 D3
Frankfurt am Main Germany
93 F3
Franz Josef Land (island
group) Russian Federation
27 F5
Fredericton New Brunswick,
Canada 53 C6, 55 D5
Freetown Sierra Leone 165 F3
Fremantle Australia 182,
183 H2
French Guiana 67 C5,
70–71, 200
French Polynesia Polynesia
25 F5, 181 C4, 200
Fresno California, U.S.A.
49 G3
Fujayrah United Arab
Emirates 133 D7
Fukuoka Japan 157 G2
Fundy, Bay of Canada 54,
55 D5

G

Gabon 159 F4, **174–175**, 192
Gaborone Botswana 177 E5
Galápagos Islands 18, 25 F7
Galilee, Sea of (lake) Israel 127 C3
Gambia 159 D1, **164–165**, 192
Ganges (river) India/ Bangladesh 19, 138, 139 D5 & C3, 140, 141 C2
Garoua Cameroon 169 F2
Gaza Israel 126, 127 E1
Gaziantep Turkey 123 E5
Gdańsk Poland 99 C5
Geelong Australia 185 H5
General Santos Philippines 147 H6
Geneva Switzerland 95 J5
Genoa Italy 97 C3
George V Land Antarctica 189 G5
Georgetown Guyana 71 C3
Georgia 115 D2, **118–119**, 192
Georgia (state) U.S.A. 31 C6, **36–37**, 196
Geraldton Australia 183 G2
Germany 81 E3, **92–93**, 192
Ghana Africa 159 E3, **166–167**, 192
Ghent Belgium 87 F3
Gibraltar Mediterranean Sea 81 G2, 91 H3, 200
Gibraltar, Strait of Morocco/ Spain 91 H3, 163 F2
Gibson Desert Australia 182, 183 E4
Gila (river) Arizona/New Mexico, U.S.A. 41 D1
Gilbert Islands 25 F3
Giza Egypt 161 E6
Giza Plateau Egypt 160
Glasgow U.K. 85 D4
Glorieuses Island (Indian Ocean) 200
Gobi Desert 19, 148, 149 E6
Godavari (river) India 139 F3
Goiânia Brazil 73 F5

Golan Heights (hilly region) Israel/Syria 125 H6, 127 C3, 201
Gold Coast Australia 185 E6
Gonder Ethiopia 170 D3
Good Hope, Cape of South Africa 19, 179 G2
Göteborg Sweden 83 G3
Graham Land Antarctica 189 D2
Grampian Mountains U.K. 85 D4
Gran Chaco South America 18, 76, 77 F5, 78, 79 C4
Grand Bahama (island) Bahamas 63 D3
Grand Canyon Arizona, U.S.A. 41 D2
Grand Rapids Michigan, U.S.A. 45 E4
Graz Austria 95 C4
Great Australian Bight Australia 19, 181 H6, 182, 183 H6, 185 G2
Great Barrier Reef Australia 180, 181 G4, 184, 185 B5
Great Basin U.S.A. 46, 47 F3
Great Bear Lake Northwest Territories, Canada 18
Great Britain 80, 84
Great Dividing Range (mountain range) Australia 19, 185 C4 & F6
Great Lakes 18 Canada 52, 54 U.S.A. 32, **44–45**
Great Plains North America 18, 42, 43 C2
Great Rift Valley Africa 19, 158, 170, 171 F3, 176
Great Salt Lake Utah, U.S.A. 47 E4
Great Sandy Desert Australia 19, 182, 183 D4
Great Slave Lake Northwest Territories, Canada 18
Great Victoria Desert Australia 19, 182, 183 F5
Greater Antilles (island group) 62, 63

Greece 81 G5, 104, **106–107**, 106, 192
Greenland (island) Arctic Ocean 13, 18, 21 C4, 26, 27 G3, 29 B5, 200
Greenland Sea 27, G4
Greensboro North Carolina, U.S.A. 39 E5
Greenville South Carolina, U.S.A. 39 E4
Grenada 29 G7, **64–65**, 192
Grossglockner (mountain) Austria 95 F4
Guadalajara Mexico 59 F5
Guadeloupe (island) Caribbean Sea 65 D5, 200
Guam (island) Micronesia 25 E2, 181 G2, 200
Guangzhou China 153 H5
Guatemala 29 H5, **60–61**, 192
Guatemala City Guatemala 61 H3
Guayaquil Ecuador 75 C2
Guayaquil, Gulf of Ecuador 75 C2
Guernsey Channel Islands, U.K. 200
Guiana Highlands 18
Guianas South America 67, **70–71**
Guinea 159 E2, **164–165**, 192
Guinea, Gulf of 19, 165 G5
Guinea-Bissau 159 E1, **164–165**, 192
Gujranwala Pakistan 137 E6
Gulf States 132–133
Guyana 67 C4, **70–71**, 192
Gyumri Armenia 119 F5

H

Hague, The Netherlands 87 D4
Haifa Israel 127 C2
Haiphong Vietnam 143 B5
Haiti 29 G6, **62–63**, 192
Halifax Nova Scotia, Canada 53 B6, 55 D5

Nampula Mozambique 177 B3
Nanjing China 153 F6
Nantes France 89 D2
Napier New Zealand 187 E6
Naples Italy 97 E5
Narmada (river) India 139 D2
Narva Estonia 109 B6
Nashville Tennessee, U.S.A. 39 E3
Nassau Bahamas 63 D3
Nauru 25 F3, 181 F3, 193
Nazareth Israel 127 C2
Nazret Ethiopia 171 E3
N'Djamena Chad 169 E3
Ndola Zambia 175 C6
Nebraska (state) U.S.A. 31 F4, 42–43, 196
Negev Desert Israel 127 G2
Negros (island) Philippines 147 F4
Nejd (desert) Saudi Arabia 129 E3
Nemunas (river) Lithuania 109 G4
Nepal 115 F4, 138–139, 193
Netherlands 81 E3, 86, 86–87, 193
Netherlands Antilles 64, 65 F3, 201
Nevada (state) U.S.A. 31 H4, 46–47, 196
New Brunswick (province) Canada 53 C6, 54–55, 197
New Caledonia (island) Melanesia 25 G3, 181 F5, 201
New Delhi India 139 C3
New England U.S.A. 32
New Hampshire (state) U.S.A. 31 B4, 32–33, 196
New Haven Connecticut, U.S.A. 33 F4
New Jersey (state) U.S.A. 31 B4, 34–35, 197
New Mexico (state) U.S.A. 31 F5, 40–41, 197
New Orleans Louisiana, U.S.A. 37 F3

New Siberian Islands (island group) Russian Federation 19, 27 D5
New South Wales (state) Australia 185 F5
New York (state) U.S.A. 31 C4, 32–33, 197
New York City New York, U.S.A. 32, 33 G4
New Zealand 180, 181 F6, 186–187, 194
    Pacific Ocean 25 G3
Newark New Jersey, U.S.A. 35 D6
Newcastle Australia 185 F6
Newcastle upon Tyne U.K. 85 E5
Newfoundland and Labrador (island) Newfoundland, Canada 21 D3, 54
Newfoundland and Labrador (province) Canada 53 C4, 54–55, 197
Niagara Falls U.S.A./Canada 55 F6
Niamey Niger 167 E3
Nicaragua 29 H5, 60–61, 194
Nicaragua, Lake Nicaragua 60, 61 F5
Nice France 89 F6
Nicobar Islands Indian Ocean 23 D5, 139 I6
Nicosia Cyprus 123 F5
Nieuw Nickerie Suriname 71 D4
Niger 159 D3, 166–167, 194
Niger (river) western Africa 19, 165 E5, 166, 167 E4
Nigeria 159 E3, 166–167, 166, 194
Niihau (island) Hawaii, U.S.A. 31 D1, 51 F1
Nile (river) Africa 13, 19, 158, 160, 161 E6, 168, 169 D5
Nis Serbia and Montenegro 105 E5
Niue (island) Polynesia 25 F4, 181 E4, 201
Nizhniy Novgorod Russian Federation 113 F3

Nizhnyaya Tunguska Russian Federation 19
Nizwā Oman 131 B3
Norfolk Virginia, U.S.A. 39 D6
Norfolk Island Pacific Ocean 25 G3, 181 F5, 201
North America 18, 25 E6, 28–29
North Cape Norway 27 G5, 83 B5
North Carolina (state) U.S.A. 31 C5, 38–39, 197
North Dakota (state) U.S.A. 31 F3, 42–43, 197
North Island New Zealand 187 E5
North Korea see Korea, North
North Magnetic Pole 27 E3
North Pole 26, 27 E4
North Sea 19, 20, 21, 81, 82, 83, 85, 86, 87, 92, 93
Northeast Africa 160–161
Northern Arabia 128–129
Northern Canada 56–57
Northern Central Africa 168–169
Northern Central Europe 98–99
Northern Ireland U.K. 84, 85 E3
Northern Mariana Islands Micronesia 25 E2, 181 G2, 201
Northern Territory (state) Australia 185 D2
Northwest Africa 162–163
Northwest Asia 122–123
Northwest Territories (province) Canada 53 H3, 56–57, 197
Norvegia, Cape Antarctica 189 C4
Norway 81 D4, 82–83, 194
Norwegian Sea 19, 21, 27, 81
Nottingham U.K. 85 F5
Nouakchott Mauritania 165 E3
Nova Scotia (province) Canada 53 B6, 54–55, 197

218

Salto Uruguay 79 D5
Salvador Brazil 73 F7
Salzburg Austria 95 E3
Samara Russian Federation
113 F4
Samarkand Uzbekistan
121 G3
Samoa (island group) 24–25,
25 F3, 181 E4, 194
Sámos (island) Greece 107 F6
San Antonio Texas, U.S.A.
41 F6
San Diego California, U.S.A.
49 H4
San Jose California, U.S.A.
49 F3
San José Costa Rica 61 E5
San Juan Puerto Rico 63 E6
San Luis Potosí Mexico
59 E5
San Marino 81 G3, 96–97,
194
San Marino San Marino
97 D4
San Miguel de Tucumán
Argentina 79 C3
San Pedro Sula Honduras
61 G3
San Salvador El Salvador
61 H4
Sanaa Yemen 131 H6
Santa Ana El Salvador 61 H4
Santa Cruz (river) Argentina
79 H3
Santa Cruz Bolivia 77 E4, 78
Santa Fe New Mexico, U.S.A.
41 D4
Santiago Chile 79 E2
Santiago Dominican Republic
63 E5
Santiago de Cuba Cuba
63 F4
Santo Domingo Dominican
Republic 63 F5
Santos Brazil 73 G5
São Francisco (river) Brazil
73 E7
São Paulo Brazil 72, 73 G5
São Roque, Cape Brazil
21 F4

São Tomé São Tomé &
Príncipe 175 H3
São Tomé (island) 175 H3
São Tomé & Príncipe 21 F6,
159 F3, 174–175, 194
Sapporo Japan 157 B6
Sarajevo Bosnia-Herzegovina
103 F6
Saratov Russian Federation
113 G3
Sardinia (island) Italy 97 F3
Saskatchewan (province)
Canada 53 G5, 56–57, 197
Saskatchewan, North (river)
Canada 57 H3
Saskatchewan, South (river)
Canada 57 H3
Saskatoon Saskatchewan,
Canada 57 H4
Saudi Arabia 115 E2,
128–129, 194
Sava (river) Croatia/Slovenia
103 C3 & E5
Savannah (river) Georgia,
U.S.A. 39 F4
Savannakhet Laos 143 D4
Sayan Mountains Russian
Federation 19
Scandinavia 80, 82–83
Scotia Sea 21, 67
Scotland U.K. 84–85, 85 D4
Scott Base Antarctica New
Zealand 189 G5
Scranton Pennsylvania, U.S.A.
35 D5
Scutari, Lake Albania 105 F3
Seattle Washington, U.S.A.
48, 48, 49 B3
Seine (river) France 89 C3 &
D4
Selenge (river) Mongolia
149 F3
Selvas Brazil 19, 73 D2
Sendai Japan 157 E6
Senegal 159 D1, 164–165,
194
Senegal (river) western Africa
165 E3
Seoul South Korea 154,
155 F4

Serbia (province) Serbia and
Montenegro 104, 104,
105 D4
Serbia and Montenegro
81 G4, 104–105, 194
Sertão Brazil 73 D7
Sevan, Lake Armenia 119 E5
Severn (river) U.K. 85 G5
Severnaya Zemlya (island
group) Russian Federation
19, 27 E5
Seville Spain 91 G3
Seychelles (island group)
22–23, 23 E3 159 F7,
194
Sfax Tunisia 163 B3
Shackleton Ice Shelf
Antarctica 189 F7
Shanghai China 153 F6
Shannon (river) Ireland
85 G2
Sharjah United Arab Emirates
133 D6
Sheffield U.K. 85 F5
Shenyang China 153 D6
Sherbrooke Quebec, Canada
55 E5
Shikoku Japan 156, 157 G3
Shīrāz Iran 135 E5
Shymkent Kazakhstan
121 F4
Siberian Lowland (plain)
Russian Federation 19,
116, 117 G5
Sicily Italy 96, 97 H5
Sicily, Strait of Italy 97 H4
Sidon Lebanon 125 I5
Sierra Leone 159 E2,
164–165, 194
Sierra Madre Occidental
(mountain range) Mexico
18, 58, 59 G3
Sierra Madre Oriental
(mountain range) Mexico
18, 58, 59 F4
Sierra Nevada (mountain
range) Spain 90, 91 G4
Sierra Nevada (mountain
range) U.S.A. 48, 49 E3
Sinai Peninsula Egypt 161 E7

Index of Countries